Living Heritage of Mewar

Living Heritage of Mewar

Architecture of the City Palace, Udaipur

Shikha Jain
Vanicka Arora

Mapin Publishing

SUPPORTED BY

Maharana of Mewar Charitable Foundation, Udaipur

First published in India in 2017 by
Mapin Publishing
in association with
Maharana Mewar Historical Publications Trust,
under the aegis of Maharana of Mewar Charitable Foundation, The City Palace, Udaipur, India

Simultaneously published in
the United States of America in 2017 by
Grantha Corporation
77 Daniele Drive, Hidden Meadows,
Ocean Township, NJ 07712
E: mapin@mapinpub.com

Distributors
North America
Antique Collectors' Club
T: +1 800 252 5231 • F: 413 529 0862
E: info@antiquecc.com
www.antiquecollectorsclub.com

United Kingdom and Europe
Gazelle Book Services Ltd.
T: +44 1 5246 8765 • F: 44 1524 63232
E: sales@gazellebooks.co.uk
www.gazellebookservices.co.uk

Thailand, Laos, Cambodia and Myanmar
Paragon Asia Co. Ltd
T: +66 2877 7755 • F: 66 2468 9636
E: info@paragonasia.com

Malaysia
Areca Books
T: +604 2610307
E: arecabooks@gmail.com

Rest of the World
Mapin Publishing Pvt. Ltd
706 Kaivanna, Panchvati, Ellisbridge,
Ahmedabad 380006 INDIA
T: +91 79 40 228 228 • F: +91 79 40 228 201
E: mapin@mapinpub.com
www.mapinpub.com

ISBN: 978-93-85360-18-3 (Mapin)
ISBN: 978-1-935677-75-8 (Grantha)
LCCN: 2016951188

Text: Dr. Shikha Jain and Vanicka Arora
Design: Designflyover Consulting LLP (DFO), Mumbai
design@designflyover.com

Editorial support: Mapin Editorial
Production: Mapin Design Studio
Printed at TWP Sdn. Bhd., Malaysia

Pages 2–3: Eastern Façade of The City Palace, Udaipur with Manek Chowk in the foreground, 1895–1905 CE, Acc No. 2009.10.0139-00045

Eternal Mewar

Custodianship unbroken since 734 AD

Maharana of Mewar Charitable Foundation (MMCF), Udaipur
Contact: Mr. Bhupendra Singh Auwa, Administrator in Chief, MMCF,
The City Palace, Udaipur 313 001, Rajasthan, India
Telephone: +91 294 241 9021 - 29 | Fax:+91 294 241 9020
mmcf@eternalmewar.in | www.eternalmewar.in

Contents

Foreword

For more than thirty years, the Getty Foundation, USA has fulfilled the philanthropic mission of the Getty Trust by supporting individuals and institutions committed to advancing the greater understanding and preservation of the visual arts in Los Angeles and throughout the world, including a number of projects in India. In 2005 and 2007, the Getty Foundation awarded two grants to the Maharana of Mewar Charitable Foundation, Udaipur, Rajasthan, India to support the phased development of a comprehensive conservation plan for the City Palace in Udaipur.

The City Palace of Udaipur is a consummate model of Mewar Rajput architecture combined with later adapted Mughal additions and is one of the most majestic palace structures in Rajasthan. To preserve this jewel for the future as well as manage the normal wear and tear of the site's many visitors, its stewards recognized the need for a complete conservation plan to guide maintenance of the site's historic features.

The project developed by the Maharana of Mewar Charitable Foundation aligned with the Getty Foundation's dedication to advancing the practice of conservation through careful research and planning. A team of conservation professionals, skillfully led by Dr. Shikha Jain, developed a master conservation plan that synthesized detailed information on the history, condition, and maintenance and conservation needs of the City Palace. Now a decade later, we are tremendously pleased with the outcome of the project, and it is rewarding to see the fruit of many years of hard work captured in this handsomely designed publication.

It is a great privilege to have supported the work for the City Palace, and we congratulate the Maharana of Mewar Charitable Foundation, Udaipur for protecting this splendid architectural complex for future generations.

Deborah Marrow

Director

The Getty Foundation

PREFACE

I am delighted to introduce this much-awaited book on The City Palace Museum. It is the first of its kind from Udaipur and is the result of the participation and efforts of a host of professionals and academicians associated with our Maharana of Mewar Charitable Foundation.

At the outset, I wish to thank all of them for their endeavour to understand the history of Mewar through the tangible heritage enshrined in The City Palace Museum—its architecture, painting and sculpture—and sharing it with global and Indian audiences in the 21st century.

In this preamble my humble attempt is to write about the spirit and ethos of Mewar, what has been termed as our 'intangible heritage'. It also carries a host of messages for new audiences who will be reading this book. I hope they will connect with the concept of custodianship as a form of governance and with 'living heritage' as a movement which is bridging the past with the future. Both these concepts have the power to meaningfully impact our worlds; and are keeping alive value systems that have been integral to our way of life, our Indian civilization, in fact.

Custodianship is a unique value system received in trust from Maharishi Harit Rashi by the founding father of our House of Mewar, Bappa Rawal, in 734 AD. We, as descendants, are proud to be upholding this cherished and time-tested principle of governance in every age.

Mahatma Gandhi in the early 20th century, during the freedom struggle, spoke about trusteeship in society. He wanted to inspire the wealthy and privileged to use their financial resources for the benefit of all people. In Mewar, the concept of trusteeship or custodianship, as distinct from ownership, had been internalized almost 1300 years earlier.

Custodians are caretakers, safe-keepers, or as some have said stewards; they are not owners. As a Custodian, it becomes my self-motivated and voluntary duty to preserve and pass on what I have received in trust to my successors. There is an enormous sense of responsibility towards the task, but there is little or no 'ownership'.

Mewar's rulers never thought of themselves as Kings but as Custodians or Diwans of Parameshwaraji Maharaj Shree Eklingnath ji, serving the people in His name. Like my forefathers, I continue to be first the Diwan of Shree Eklingnath ji and then the 76th Custodian of the House of Mewar.

Nothing has changed over the centuries; even though everything in our world has changed!

Custodian's perspective

From our perspective as Custodians, we see a panorama of historical events which impacted our lives in different ways; sometimes putting into jeopardy the very survival of the House of Mewar itself.

The Preface is our 'inside-out' perspective, giving readers glimpses of how Mewar has withstood the tests of time not just in the 20th century but also in every preceding century. Each era posed major challenges for the Maharanas of Mewar as Custodians and threatened their independence and sense of identity.

During the mighty empire of the Mughals, the Maratha invasions, the British Imperial Rule and in the Republic of India, there were innumerable occasions when Mewar's resilience was tested. Mewar managed to survive, often against all odds, and succeeded to move ahead with their sense of pride and honour intact: We can witness the transition from the Kingdom of Mewar in the 8th and 9th centuries to the Princely State of Mewar in the 19th and 20th centuries and now the House of Mewar, the world's oldest-serving dynasty.

As we read this book today, and turn its pages to marvel at the sights of The City Palace Museum, we need to pay our tribute to 23 generations of Maharanas of Mewar who have contributed to the development and sustainability of Udaipur since 1559, often in very hostile external environments. Without their abiding commitment, their achievements big and small, and the platforms they consciously built, we would not be able to experience and enjoy The City Palace Museum as we are doing so today.

We may not realize it today but each generation of Maharanas was conscious of the need to preserve and conserve the heritage they had received in trust. The preservation and conservation were done in the best possible manner. Court and administrative records were also meticulously maintained and were preserved for posterity. Maharana Mewar Research Institute, to provide an example, is one such repository of invaluable records relating to Mewar and Udaipur over the last 300 years.

Being the 76th Custodian of the House of Mewar I feel humbled by the foresight and endeavours of my illustrious ancestors, many of whom were not formally educated, in the way we understand education today. But they demonstrated their innate wisdom, sensitivity towards history and gave priority to preservation and archiving of records in The City Palace.

Moreover, they remained steadfast to the value system which emphasized the five values of honour, self-reliance, independence, service to and respect for all humanity. This, in essence, is the overarching responsibility of discharging the Custodian's duties. And I am happy to say it continues till date.

This book is our respectful dedication to the generations of Maharanas of Mewar to whom we pay our heartfelt tributes.

Repository of memories

When I think of The City Palace Museum, I think of it as a 'home, a place of residence'; never as a museum or as a unique cultural heritage site. It is first and foremost a repository of memories for me more than anything else: it is where I grew up, studied and played with friends.

The City Palace remains a familiar and much-loved place of residence for the family members of the House of Mewar and the extended clans. It witnessed marriages and births and festivities: the entire cycle of life events that were celebrated and cherished by all.

The City Palace was where my father, as the young Maharaj Kumar Bhagwat Singh, brought home his bride, Maharaj Kumari Sushila Kumari of Bikaner, in full regalia. My parents settled down in a refurbished area of the Zenana Mahal in 1940. I felt especially privileged and moved, in 2009–10, to dedicate their 'apartment area' as the Bhagwat Prakash Photo Gallery, showcasing the rare and archival photographs from our archives.

I can visualise even earlier times when my revered grandfather, His Highness Maharana Bhupal Singh, was the 74th Custodian, governing the Princely State of Mewar through the tumultuous 1940s, when few could have foreseen the traumatic events about to overtake India as a colony of the British Empire and, then, as a new republic in 1947.

The City Palace, till India's Independence in 1947 was the seat of Mewar's government, the hub of administration, a focal point for social and cultural activities which emanated from here and involved all communities and people of Udaipur and Mewar. It was an entire and complete world in itself, fuelled by its ancient spiritual and religious values, governed by its own protocols and humanitarian spirit which distinguished Mewar and Udaipur for centuries.

At the time of India's Independence, the State of Mewar, relatively untouched by the traumas of Partition, became the first Princely State to integrate with the Union of India. It was a voluntary act reflecting the deep understanding of Mewar that a strong and unified India was more important than mere regional independence.

Maharana Bhupal Singh, the Custodian of Mewar in 1947, said on that historic occasion, "Today is a day of which I am extremely proud. India is independent. It brings to fulfilment our 1400-year struggle and the endeavour of my forefathers. It becomes my sacred duty to merge our cherished and sacred Flame of Freedom with that of free and independent Union of India."

These words have not lost their meaning even today; they resonate with power and positive energy for me in the 21st century. Maharana Bhupal Singh's austere lifestyle and places of residence in The City Palace can be seen by visitors to the Museum today.

Defining Udaipur

For the learned academicians, architects, historians and researchers who are 'looking in from the outside', The City Palace Museum is often seen as a series of palaces and courtyards—they calibrate evolution of architectural styles and make us aware of spaces both private and public. They study paintings and are able to deduce changes in artistic and design styles; the lives of painters and the equipment they used become important.

Their journey into Mewar's rich heritage is fascinating and endless, if you ask me, as it keeps throwing up new challenges of how to assess the tangible heritage. It also points to the importance of understanding the intangible heritage, the 'software', the ethos which made possible the creation of Mewar's built heritage and its magnificence in the arts.

There are two facets which I would like to draw the reader's attention.

One is the 'open-ness' of Mewar's cultural ethos, the innate ability to respect other cultures, traditions and religious practices and also to promote and protect them whenever required. This respect for others stems from both a sense of humility and a sense of confidence.

Mewar, through the ages, was a confluence of cultures where priests, poets, painters and pioneers in different fields would be given their due reward as they made their contribution to existing ideas and projects. This open-ness never resulted in Mewar losing or diluting its own heritage; rather it was the absorption of the new that embellished, nourished the existing culture.

The second facet is closely linked to the first; it is the 'quest for excellence'.

Mewar's Custodians may not have been larger-than-life personalities, like some of their peers, but they created a cultural environment where talent and creativity flourished, generation after generation. The result is there for us to witness in the expanse of Udaipur's City Palace—be it Mardana and Zenana Mahals or Shiv Niwas Palace, Fateh Prakash Palace, Jagmandir Island Palace and the Jag Niwas Palace (now Lake Palace Hotel).

Though these palaces and island–palaces have been built in different eras, from the seventeenth to the early twentieth century, across a span of almost 450 turbulent years, there is an authenticity and a degree of originality in these palaces which continues to amaze us till today. (There are also several engineering marvels embedded in these palaces but that is another story.)

Even a lay person can experience the architectural uniqueness of these palaces, the aesthetic continuity and integration into The City Palace as a whole. Each palace exemplifies a quest for excellence that has withstood the arduous tests of time and, in the process, has become iconic.

Excellence ensures a certain degree of timelessness and it clearly demonstrates Mewar's commitment to this awe-inspiring ethic. This book is, in many ways, capturing the 'quest for excellence' in its pages.

Living Heritage

Through The City Palace Museum, and under the aegis of our Foundation, our focus is on preserving the 'living heritage' of Mewar. Living heritage is a constantly evolving model of managing heritage, keeping it alive, dynamic and relevant to changing times. It covers both the intangible and tangible forms of heritage.

I firmly believe living heritage has the inherent dynamism to trigger development of modern facilities in ancient environments. This development leads to enrichment of local economies, enhancement of quality of life in communities, higher employment generation, stemming of the rural migration to urban areas and generating greater pride in traditional professions, crafts and culture. It injects dignity in heritage and enriches the societal fabric. Living heritage, thus, bestows a distinct identity to those who live by its values and principles and celebrate its authenticity every day.

Unfortunately, India has not been able to showcase its heritage to power tourism. We are still stuck in the paradigms of the past, where tourism is considered. While tourism globally has gone through a sea-change, in India we seem to follow the model of sermonizing and not sharing. Our focus on tourism is restricted to forts, palaces and temples.

In India, we are blessed with the widest variety of opportunities to power tourism. The time has come to change our model, our mindset in our tourism promotion policies, if we want to become globally competitive in powering tourism and thereby improving the economy of our nation. There are innumerable examples of nations, who are dependent on, and thriving on, tourism despite having far limited opportunities and resources as compared to us.

At the same time, it is important to preserve the past. If we do not do so, then our legacies will be obliterated from the face of this earth and remain available only to scholars. It is, therefore, imperative that we continue to spread the awareness, particularly amongst the next generation, so that it is not just the modern with which they are comfortable but also the past of which they are an integral part.

We are not interested in evoking the feudal past in today's time and age of globalization. We are invoking an appreciation of our 'living heritage'. If we do not subscribe to this, we would be losing our identity as Indians and become mere robotic clones of other cultures and civilizations. In my opinion no one in our country would wish that to happen.

May the blessings of Parameshwaraji Maharaj Shree Eklingnath ji, the Supreme Ruler of Mewar, continue to be showered on all those who tirelessly worked to create this book, the visitors to our Museum, the city of Udaipur and onto our entire world.

Arvind Singh Mewar
Chairman and Managing Trustee
Maharana of Mewar Charitable Foundation

The Palace
Udaipur 313001 Rajasthan, India
www.eternalmewar.in

Architecture, Culture and Patronage

Maharana as a Trustee of his Kingdom

The origin of the Sisodia Rajputs, the rulers of Mewar dates back to 734 AD. Bappa Rawal of the Guhil lineage founded the Mewar Dynasty. As the founder, Bappa Rawal made a solemn promise to his Guru, Maharishi Harit Rashi that he and his descendants would protect and fulfill the sacred trusteeship of Shree Eklingnath ji (a manifestation of Lord Shiva) who would be the real ruler of Mewar. As direct descendants of Bappa Rawal, all the rulers of Mewar are hereditary custodians of Mewar on behalf of Shree Eklingnath ji. The shrine of Eklingnath ji is located about 22 km north of Udaipur, the last capital of erstwhile Mewar, This shrine is protected and worshipped by the royal family and people of Mewar region till date. This principle of 'kingship' as 'trusteeship' formed the basis for governance of the state of Mewar and continues to reflect in the maintenance and protection of the City Palace at Udaipur today.

The first capital of Mewar was Chittorgarh, which remained the seat of power for several successive generations until 1553 AD, when the new capital of Udaipur was founded by Maharana Udai Singh II. The City Palace at Udaipur has seen continued patronage; even as its earlier administrative and residential role came to an end with democratic India, the custodianship is continued under the Maharana of Mewar Charitable Foundation. This aspect reflects in the way the site is used, maintained or taken care of, with the best known contemporary approaches as well as a continuity of traditional processes. The City Palace is significant for continuity of traditional building crafts and technology; few craftsmen associated with the palace have been retained over generations enabling this continuity. Most traditions associated with the life of the royal family are retained in palace spaces such as the annual celebration of festivals of Ashwa Poojan, Kartik Poornima and Holika Dahan, which see broader participation by the citizens too.

The tradition of patronizing the arts and crafts of the region continues, as the palace is a venue for annual arts and crafts market such as 'Rang'. In fact, introduction of new events validate the historic site's importance in the present day context. The royal family continues linkages with the site as patrons and users of the site. The temples within the complex are worshipped by the royal family till today and several traditional rituals are carried out in the palace and museum spaces, thus truly making it a Living Heritage Site.

Architectural Evolution of the City Palace

The City Palace is a unique example of the 16th century palace-fortress typology that emerged in medieval Rajasthan. This type evolved from the earlier fort structures that were usually spread over a large hill top and housed palaces, including defense infrastructure and settlements. Some of these are the earlier forts of the Mewar rulers such as Chittorgarh and Kumbhalgarh. The City Palace differs from them as it is more like a palace complex on the hill with the city of Udaipur spread below within a city wall. The fortress like appearance of this palace is achieved by encasing the hill with a retaining wall on which the palaces stand so that it seems to rise to a monumental height and has a continuous fortress like facade along the hill.

Despite the existence of several layers of intervention since the 16th century, the spatial planning of the palace shows a continuity of courtyard planning till the turn of the 19th century. The spatial planning of the City Palace is reflected in the interlinked courtyards at various levels on the original hill. As typical of any spatial planning in the Indian context - it is the innermost courtyards usually located at higher points that function as private areas, whereas the outer ones at lower levels are the more public courtyards. It is interesting to observe the architectural evolution of the City Palace under different rulers, in which built spaces were typically constructed around a central open space that acted as significant 'punctuations' in the intricate mosaic of the palace architecture and important links in its spatial articulation.

The size of these opens spaces called *chowks*, which literally means four-sided courtyards, varied according to usage depending on whether it is the ruler's private *durbar* (royal court) or a large gathering ground for the public to hold all kinds of group activities - social, religious, recreational and sports. These courtyards were vital to the functioning of the palace and sometimes have been designed as actual gardens complete with trees, shrubs, flowers and fountains. These were, and still remain, as actual identifiable units along which movement and space planning were organised. Other features which delineate different spaces within the City Palace are the entrance gateways or *pols* that serve as the main public access points. These are supplemented by smaller gateways known as *deodhis* that demarcate transition spaces into smaller or more private courtyards.

Within the interiors of the City Palace, the Mardana (men's quarters) and Zenana (women's quarters) sections form the two distinct areas. The palace spaces in the Mardana include spaces such as the *darikhanas* which were the gathering space for the ruler and nobles, *mahals* which were the palatial rooms usually on the upper level and *chitrashalis* that were the semi-covered painted galleries for the rulers to use as leisure galleries. The palatial spaces were also called Vilas, Niwas and Prakash (local terms relating to the place of stay). The covered spaces opening into a court were also called *chopad*. The palace of the queens and her coterie known as the Zenana or the *rawla* and also had separate *chopad* spaces for each queen. Besides, it contained religious spaces as *mandirs* (temples) and the *osara*, as semi-covered veranda space for prayers and rituals.

The City Palace has several layers of historicity and architectural styles. The stylistic trends show influences from contemporary developments in architecture and yet are distinctly individualistic to the particular ruler of that period. Since few of the royal rulers continued to rule and construct over the turn of the centuries, it is difficult to categorise the architectural styles by each century. In total, 13 distinct layers of historic fabric are clearly visible in the architectural collage of the palace that can be possibly further categorised in five major phases that link the geography, history and social life with the architectural evolution of the site.

Phase 1 - Mewar-Mature Phase (1559-1620 AD)
Phase 2 - Mewar-Mughal Early Phase (1620-1698 AD)
Phase 3 - Mewar-Mughal Mature Phase (1698 -1778 AD)
Phase 4 - Mewar-British Phase (1778-1930 AD)
Phase 5 - Post-independence Mewar Phase (from 1931 AD)

The paintings and artwork within the City Palace are a visual record of it's evolving form.

Phases of Evolution

Phase 1

Amar Mahal dome

Rai Angan coloumn and beam niche

Mewar Mature Phase

Phase 2

Zenana Mahal dome

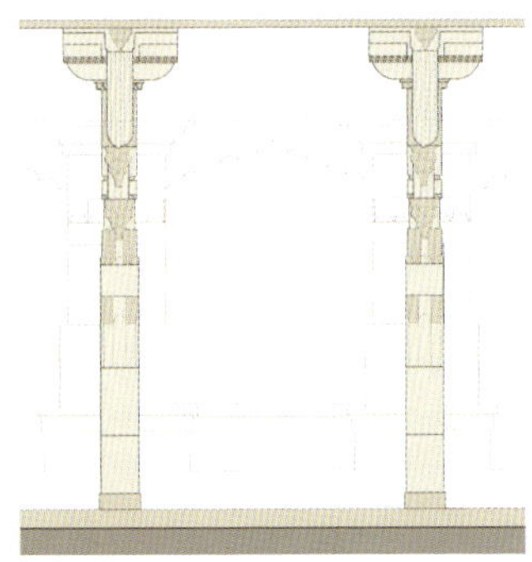

Zenana Mahal column and niche

Mewar - Mughal Early Phase

Phase 3

Baadi Mahal dome

Baadi Mahal column and niche

Mewar - Mughal Mature Phase

Phase 4

Tripoliya dome

Zenana Mahal window

Mewar - British Phase

Palace Architecture in Paintings and Maps

Dating back to 1700 AD, this is the earliest extant painting featuring the City Palace. It illustrates the evolution of the palace skyline towards the end of the second phase of the palace's evolution, the Mewar-Mughal Early Phase. Based on its representation of the architectural composition around the Manek Chowk at the beginning of the 18th century it shows several key spaces that were built by this time. The Manek Chowk itself emerged as one of the central public courtyards of the City Palace, as can be seen in this painting, which clearly focuses on the scale and activity that characterises the courtyard even today. The various gateways or *pols* and courtyards that were built by this period are clearly demarcated, and include the Badi Pol with its *dalans* on both sides and the kothar area with a courtyard in the upper right corner with all its architectural details. A gate and wall can be observed in the same location as the present day Tripoliya though the existing Tripoliya belongs to a later phase. The older gateway near the Kothar area is shown in line with Tripoliya, as it exists today. A lower portion in the middle right area shows the presence of a bailkhano (stables for animals). A gate stands in the same location as the Suraj Pol (*lower left corner*) as does a structure on the present site of Palki khana. A comparison with later period paintings show that these areas were extensively modified in succeeding phases. The Toran Pol is crowned with a huge dome (seen here in the upper left corner) which was later concealed to result in its present day appearance. The Sabha Shiromani exists as a single storied colonnaded space to the right of the Toran Pol reminiscent of the Sabha spaces in Chittorgarh. The main palace building is shown with an entrance gate with two storeys and the Rai Angan block is topped by the Dilkhushal Mahal. The Baadi Mahal on the upper right of the painting shows the palace structure in white and the encased hillock in red, thus clearly differentiating the retaining wall that encases the hill on which the palace stands. A water pond can be seen to the right of the composition, below the Baadi Mahal.

Facing Page: Maharana Amar Singh II and his court attending an animal fight in front of the Palace. c. 1705 (painting on cloth).

This painting shows the addition of a Mughal style garden with water channels to the right below the Baadi Mahal where the water pond had existed in 1700 AD.

Image Courtesy: Media Office, Eternal Mewar, The City Palace, Udaipur, Rajasthan

Above: Earliest extant painting featuring the City Palace, Udaipur. 1700 AD

Image Courtesy: Media Office, Eternal Mewar, The City Palace, Udaipur, Rajasthan

Celebrations in Manek Chowk Maharana Sangram Singh II's reign (1710–1734 AD)

These paintings which date to the reign of Maharana Sangram Singh II show the palace structures around Manek Chowk and also provide an additional view of Moti Chowk and Satanavari Paiga behind it. The first composition shows a seated Maharana Sangram Singh watching *jethi* wrestlers fighting in Manek Chowk. Earlier records mention that *jethi* wrestling was a weekly event at the City Palace. The major architectural additions of this period can be seen illustrated in the painting. The construction of the Tripoliya as the main entrance gate to Manek Chowk is seen on the extreme right of the painting. The *torans* and Nakkarkhana on Suraj Pol can also be observed on the lower left corner. Naginabadi ka Darikhana, a Mughal style garden, was created in front of the Sabha Shiromani and the Hathi ki Agad was constructed as can be seen in the right corner (below Baadi Mahal) replacing the earlier garden built by Maharana Amar Singh I. In the second painting (*below*), the composition shows the Maharana celebrating the birth of his grand-son Pratap Singh II in 1724 AD . The painting shows the addition of the Badi Chitrashali as another storey above the entrance where the Maharana is seated.

Facing Page: Maharana Sangram Singh II and Durga Das Rathore of Jodhpur watching jethi wrestlers at Manek Chowk, The City Palace, Udaipur, 1715-1720 CE, Acc. No: 2012.19.0028.

Left: Maharana Sangram Singh II celebrating the birth of Bhanwar Pratap Singh at Manek Chowk, The City Palace, Udaipur, Acc. No: 2011.18.0038

Maharana Ari Singh attending an elephant fight at the City Palace during Navratri.
Artist: Bhima and Kesuram
c. 1765
Acc. No. 2012.19.0034

Late 18th Century Map of the City Palace

A map found in the Kapad Dwara collection of the City Palace Museum, Jaipur, shows interesting details of the City Palace, Udaipur and throws light on the names of each area or space was known by in the 18th century. It is on the basis of this historic document from Maharana Ari Singh's reign that it can be acertained that the Suraj Pol was earlier known as the Samaali Pol and that the *bailkhano* (stable) was located on the lake facing side of the Zenana Mahal. It also marks Mukut Mandir Ghum showing that the structure predates Maharana Jawan Singh.

A reinterpretation of a map of the City Palace drawn in 1765 AD indicating the extents of the palace and its various courtyards. (Original map is in Kapad Dwara collection, City Palace, Jaipur).

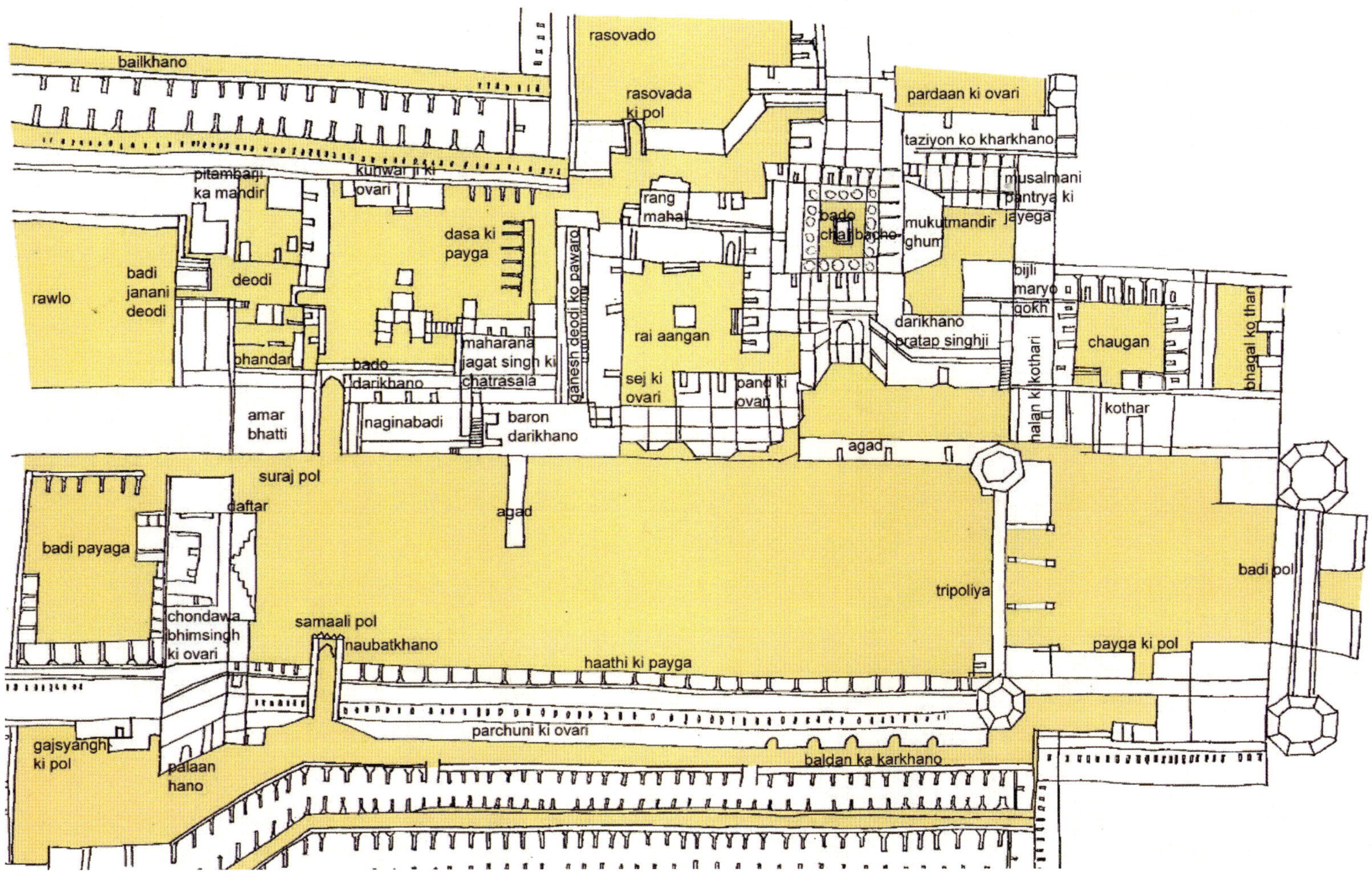

Maharana Swarup Singh playing Holi in Manek Chowk (1851 AD)

This painting highlights the architectural contributions of Maharana Swarup Singh during the 19th century. The addition of the Hawa Mahal, which is a series of screens and jaalis above Tripoliya can be seen on the right hand corner of the painting. The addition of Khush Mahal, a palace block to the right behind the Baadi Mahal can also be seen. Additions to the Toran Pol, which changed its appearance significantly from previous phases, can be observed in the top left corner of the composition. The addition of two storeys of Surya Prakash and Swarup Vilas above the Sabha Shiromani block is also evident. Smaller changes to the palace spaces can be seen in the form of stylistic alterations to the Mardana Deodhi. The painting itself documents Maharana Swarup Singh playing Holi on horseback in Manek Chowk in 1851 AD. Holi continues to be a central festival at the City Palace and involves an elaborate series of festivities attended by the royal family and locals.

RIGHT: Maharana Swarup Singh playing Holi on horse back at Manek Chowk, The City Palace, Udaipur, March 1851 A.D, Acc. No: 2012.19.0012

Ashwa Poojan at the Manek Chowk during reign of Maharana Bhupal Singh (1939 AD)

This painting is relatively recent, dating to 1939 AD and represents the palace facade as it exists today. The skyline of Manek Chowk shows minor modifications to the Mardana Deodhi and to the parapets of the Baadi Mahal terrace. This section of the palace remains more or less unchanged in the following years, and the Manek Chowk continues to be at the heart of all public festivities in the City Palace today. Seen here is the Ashwa Poojan being celebrated during the reign of Maharana Bhupal Singh.

LEFT: Maharana Bhupal Singh of Udaipur inspecting the royal horses and elephants on Ashwa-Gaj Poojan at Manek Chowk, The City Palace, Udaipur, 1939 CE, Acc. No: 2011.18.0026

Maharana Udai Singh seeking blessings of Goswami Prem Giriji Maharaj to lay the foundation of the palace at Udaipur.
Image courtesy: An exhibition titled 'Maharana Pratap—The Bravest of the Brave' mounted by FACT–India.

The Founding of a New Capital

Mewar Mature Phase

The City Palace at Udaipur has evolved as the seat of twenty two successive generations of rulers of Mewar, beginning with Maharana Udai Singh II (1537-1572 AD), the fifty-third ruler of the Mewar dynasty credited with the founding of Udaipur in the mid 16th century AD. The earlier capital of Chittor was in a vulnerable position, having suffered repeated attacks from the Mughals, the rulers at Gujarat, Malwa and even the neigbouring state of Marwar. It was in 1553 AD that work on constructing a new capital was commenced in the Girwa portion of Mewar, which was securely positioned within the Aravalli hills. The period from the reign of Maharana Udai Singh II (r.1537-1572 AD) up to that of Maharana Amar Singh I (r. 1597-1620 AD), marks an important political move in the history of Mewar. It also delineates a distinct phase in the construction of the City Palace at Udaipur, characterised by the Mewar style of architecture.

Selection of a Site

The selection of the site of the City Palace is based on the prescribed guidelines in the traditional architectural treatise of Mewar, the *Rajvallabha* by *Sutradhar* Mandan. According to this, the ideal location of a royal stronghold is best located on a fish shaped hill, called Rana Magri, next to an ample supply of water and strategically placed so as to maximise natural defenses. Perhaps his own experience in the earlier forts of Chittorgarh and Kumbhalgarh had illustrated to Maharana Udai Singh II the disadvantages of locating a fort atop a single hill. In the event of a prolonged attack, rations and supplies could run out rapidly, making the fort easy prey to invaders. Therefore, having a vast expanse of flat, arable land within the walled city and a constant supply of fresh water in the form of a lake, which also had cultivable shores ensured long term self reliance. Due to its basic geological formation, the site provided ample structural stability. The easy availability of stone and other construction materials in nearby areas was an added advantage.

RIGHT: The City Palace on the banks of Lake Pichola

Maharana Udai Singh II
AD 1537 - 1572

Maharana Pratap I
AD 1572 - 1597

Maharana Amar Singh I
AD 1597 - 1620

Strategically located on the crest of a ridge, the palace was to have its back to Lake Pichola on the west and the city towards its eastern edge. Being the highest point closest to the lake shore offered an excellent vantage point as well as adequate defence from the enemy and local wildlife. The historic 14th century water body at the village of Picholi was protected and expanded to sustain the later settlement of Udaipur. Records suggest that the small existing lake was dug deeper and wider and surrounded with bunds or *pals* to capture water run-off and use it for irrigation. The banks and shores along the palace and the rest of the city were developed into attractive *ghat*s that served as spaces for recreation and religious ceremonies. As part of an extensive defensive strategy, the Udai Sagar Lake was also constructed at this time and used systematically along with the other lakes to irrigate gardens and farmlands through an intricate system of canals. The historic text *Amar Kaavya* records various construction works undertaken by Udai Singh II; a temple behind Chogan area in Udaipur, houses for the nobles, Nauchowki in the centre of Udaipur and an incomparable palace in the Lake Pichola named the Damdama Mahal (a pre-cursor to the Jagmandir).

Some of the longest enduring socio-cultural beliefs associated with Mewar may be traced back to the founding of the new capital. According to one such legend, Maharana Udai Singh II stumbled upon the site for his new capital by a fortuitous accident, while he was hunting near Lake Pichola. He shot an arrow through a hare, which was bathed in miraculous light, which the king took to be a sign that his new city should be built at this spot. He met the revered hermit Goswami Prem Giriji Maharaj who blessed him and announced that his new capital would be prosperous and well protected. The exact location where Maharana Udai Singh II was hunting, before he met Prem Giriji was demarcated with a wooden post driven into the ground, and became known as 'Bhairav' marked till date at the entrance gateway to the palace, the Badi Pol. The site where the hermit Prem Giriji meditated became the genius loci of the palace as well as the city of Udaipur as the Nauchowki Mahal.

Beyond such social beliefs, he needs to be credited for his ingenuity in selecting a land in the Girwa valley that was well known to his ancestors for centuries for its rich natural, mineral and geological resources including Zawar and Ahar areas.

After the founding of the new capital, several new structures were built in the city, such as the Debari Gate, a *sarai* for travelers and visitors to the city, a *baori* (stepwell) as well as the Dumdama Palace on an island in the Lake Pichola. Strategically located cannons were placed on the peak of the Machla Magra (the literal translation of which means "fish shaped hillock") as well. While Udai Singh's primary focus was the building of his new capital and the strengthening of his kingdom, political strife with Marwar, Gujarat and other neighbours as well as the Mughals continued right until his death in Gogunda in 1572 AD.

Facing Page Left: Battle of Haldi Ghati (18th June 1576), 1935, Acc. No: 2011.26.0016

Facing Page Right: Kunwar Amar Singh produced Begum Khan Khana, captured in battle, before Maharana Pratap who in all magnanimity asked him to return her with respect to her camp. 1920-1930 CE, Acc. No: 2011.26.0022

Conflicts with the Mughals

Maharana Udai Singh II was succeeded by his favoured son Maharana Pratap Singh (r. 1572-1597 AD) who holds a special place in the annals not just of Mewar, but of contemporary India as a whole for his spirited resistance against the might of the Mughal Empire during the reign of Emperor Akbar. Between 1576 AD and 1585 AD, Pratap foiled several expeditions headed by Mughal generals. By 1583 AD western Mewar was back under Pratap's control. Between 1585 AD and up to his death in January 1597 AD, he succeeded in recovering substantive parts of Mewar from the Mughals. Ordinary people who had migrated out of Mewar during the turbulent years of Mewar-Mughal confrontation began to drift back to the land. Agricultural activity picked up, assisted by a series of good monsoon years, and so, albeit cautiously, did trade and economic activities. Undoubtedly the most heroic figure in the dynasty of Mewar, he never stayed in Udaipur giving up palatial luxuries in order to build his army in the wilderness. Hence, no additions of the City Palace are attributed to his reign.

Maharana Pratap's son, Amar Singh I(r. 1597-1620 AD), ascended the *gaddi* of Mewar in January 1597 AD, and set about re-organizing the various branches of administration, since governance and the structure of the state had borne the impact of the Imperial action against Maharana Pratap. During his reign, they had come to an understanding with the Mughals. Following Akbar's death, his successor, Emperor Jahangir, sent several campaigns against Mewar. Another of the Emperor's sons, Prince Khurram (the future Emperor Shah Jahan), was given the charge of leading a fresh campaign against Mewar. Amar Singh I along with his nobles and chiefs did not wish to prolong a state of affairs that was damaging to the prosperity, human resources, and economic and political well-being of Mewar. Thus, Prince Khurram was approached and peace terms were negotiated. The peace-terms were unhesitatingly approved by Emperor Jahangir and finally, an Imperial *'farman'* (or document recording the Emperor's command or order) was issued and handed over to Amar Singh I at Gogunda by Prince Khurram on 5th February 1615 AD. Mewar's prolonged confrontation with the Mughal Empire was over, at least for a while.

The rest of Amar Singh's reign was occupied with measures to rebuild Mewar. By the time Maharana Amar Singh I died in January 1620 AD, steps to improve the administration had been effectively put in place. Simultaneously, programmes for the general rehabilitation of the displaced populace, affected by the all too frequent fighting between Mewar and the imperial forces, were beginning to yield positive results. Amar Singh had moved back to the City Palace in Udaipur, and extended the palace by adding the Amar Mahal and the Bhandar Chowk as well as undertaking several smaller changes to the palace structures.

Beginnings of the Palace

The architectural form and style of this phase that has its genesis in the earlier Mewar precedents of the Kumbha Palace at Chittorgarh and Kumbhalgarh is best represented by the palace structures of the Nauchowki Mahal. These spaces reflect the planning principles, structure and architectural styles of what may be termed as the Mewar Mature Phase. These structures in the palace are of the highest architectural and archaeological significance. The landscape elements of this phase such as the Rai Angan are clearly influenced by Maharana Udai Singh's childhood recollections of Kumbha Mahal at Kumbhalgarh. The Amar Mahal with its intricate stone carved niches and vaulted chambers, is an architectural masterpiece of this era.

Left: Maharana Kumbha's Palace in Chittorgarh

Below: The City Palace skyline in its first phase

Facing Page: The first phase of development within the City Palace

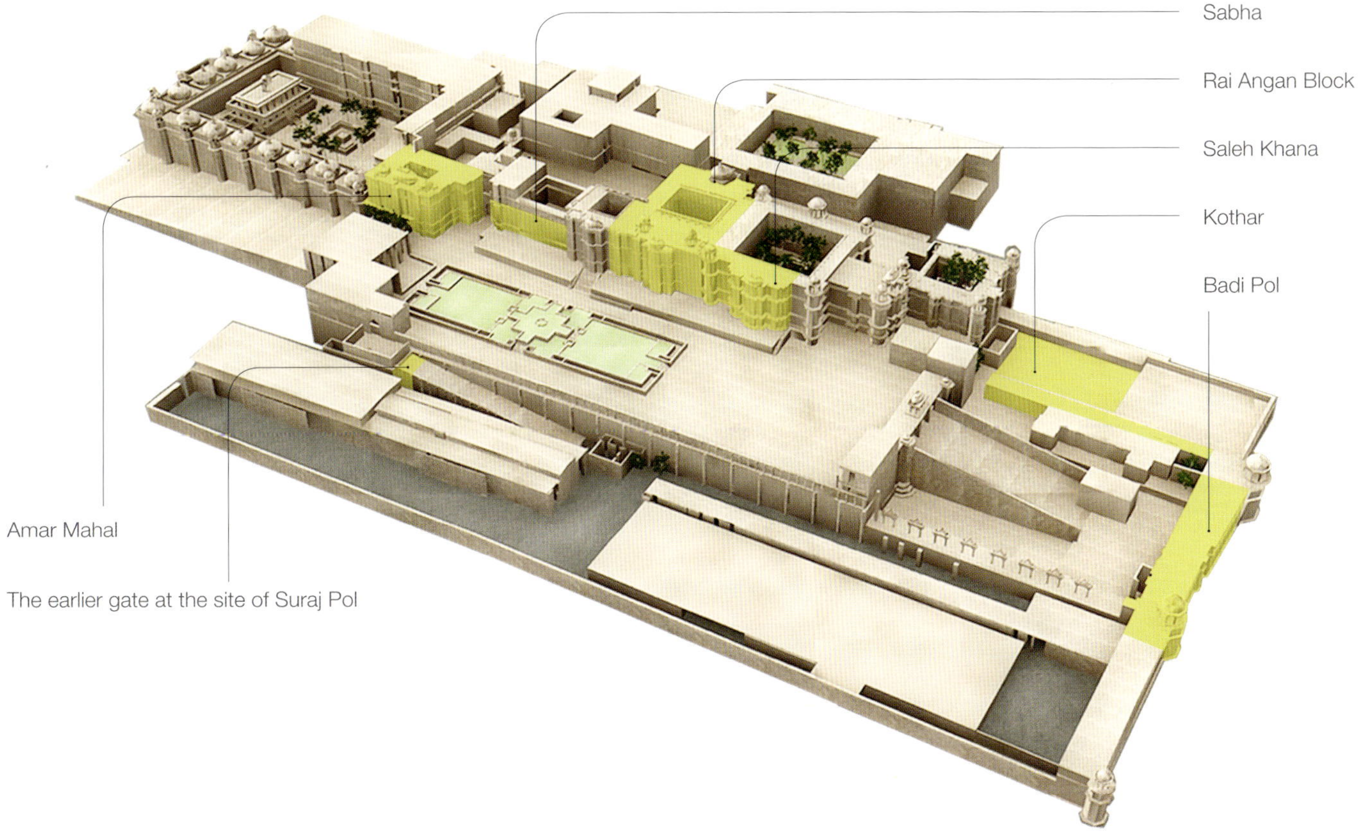
Sabha
Rai Angan Block
Saleh Khana
Kothar
Badi Pol
Amar Mahal
The earlier gate at the site of Suraj Pol

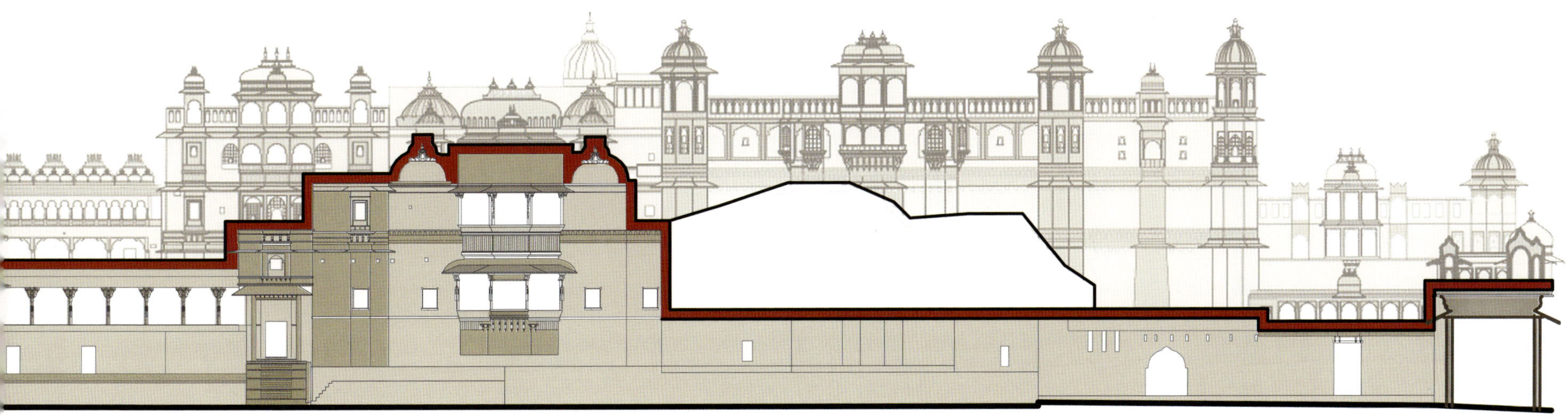

Salehkhana, Sabha and Rai Angan (Mardana)

The chronological sequence of spaces begins from Rai Angan, the genius loci of the entire City Palace as well as of the city of Udaipur. Within Rai Angan, the first and foremost palace blocks to be constructed on the hill were the Nauchowki (nine grid square room), where the priest Premgiri had resided; and the block opposite it called the Nika ki Chopad. The enclosure they formed came to be known as the Rai Angan—the courtyard for all royal rituals and coronation ceremonies. The historic text *Veer Vinod* mentions the initial construction of this palace structure and also specifies that this was the private courtyard of Maharana Udai Singh II while what is now referred to as the Salehkhana area, located below the Nika ki Chopad was the more public *mardana* section. It also mentions that the royal ladies were initially housed in a temporary structure constructed to the north of Rai Angan on the site of the existing Kothar (the block now used as office spaces).

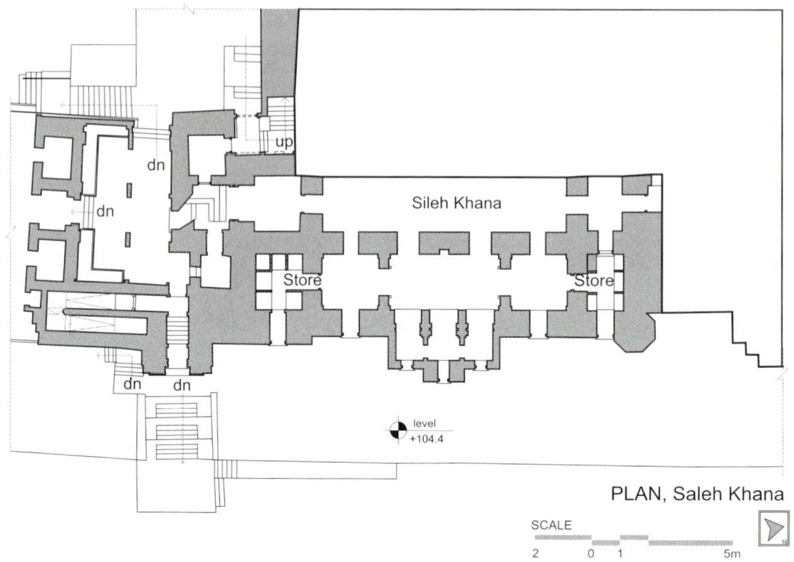

Top: Plan of Salehkhana
Above: Rai Angan

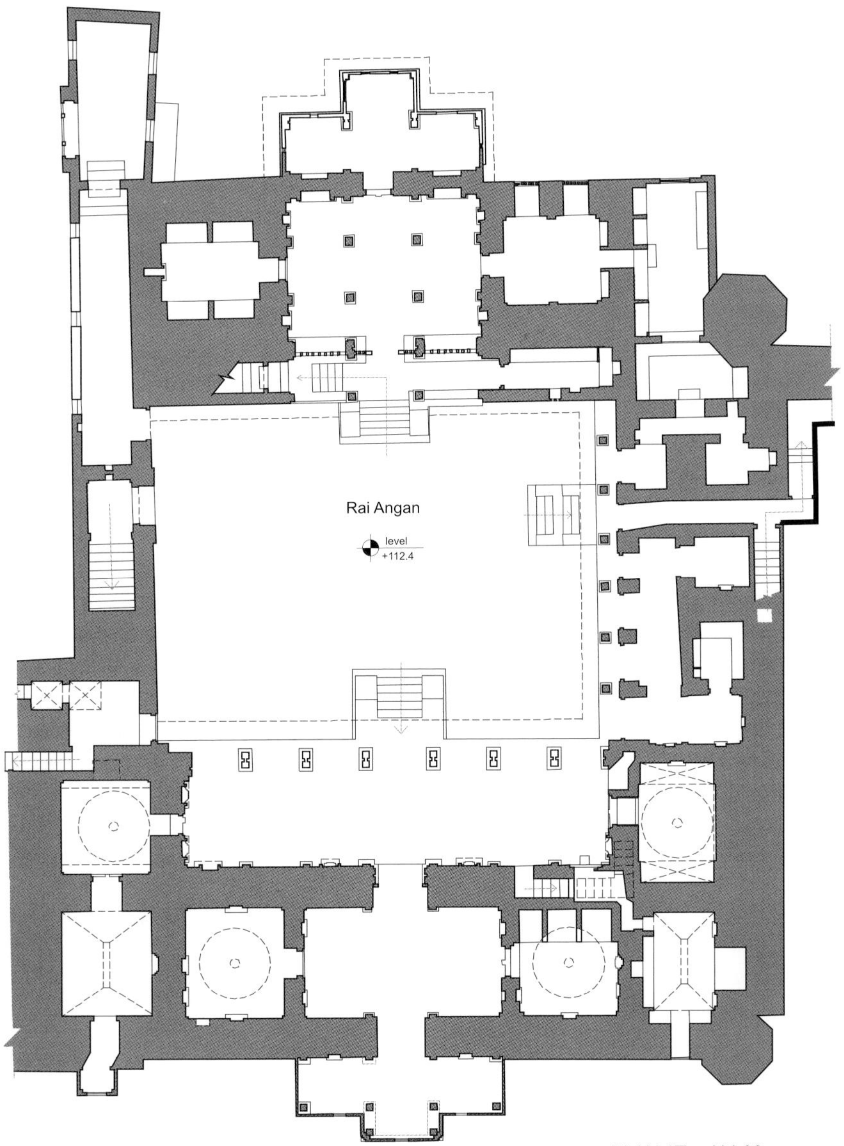

PLAN AT + 114.00m

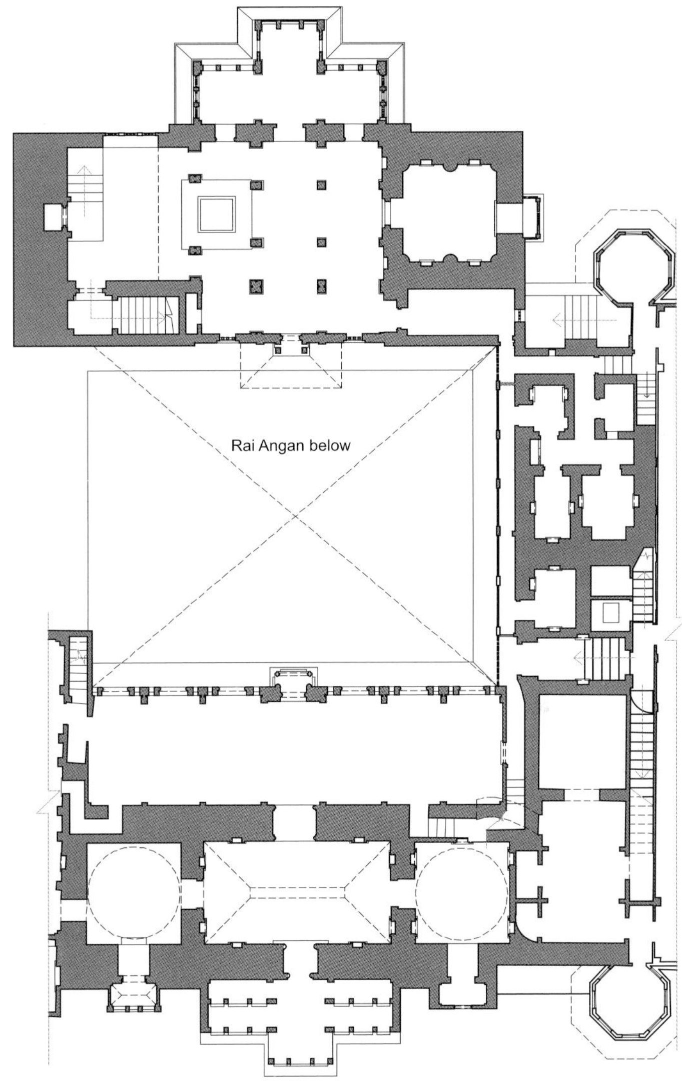

PLAN AT + 120.00m

SCALE
2 0 1 5m

Plans of Rai Angan

The nine-grid space of the Nauchowki Mahal still retains the *dhuni* (fire-pit) of Prem Giriji, in the central square kept alight by a priest. Visitors to the museum often show their reverence to this space and to the hermit by offering coins. The Nauchowki is surrounded by smaller rooms including the *panera* (water storage) to the north and the original *rasoda* (kitchen) to the south. The eastern façade is flanked by a semi-covered columnar verandah. The earlier structure of Nauchowki would have originally been a more temporary form with sloping roof as seen in the Kumbha palace at Kumbhalgarh. The nine grid space in the center is marked by intricately carved temple type stone columns and the verandah space outside has similar columns and beams supported by brackets and a stone *chajja.* This portion shows three distinct layers of historic fabric, the first layer being the original columns and brackets from 16th century. The second layer from 17th century includes the steps on the sides and the infill walls between the stone columns, with the central cusped arch opening. Similar infills are observed on the western lakeside façade. The parapet with floral motifs is an 18th century addition.

The Nika ki Chopad is a semi-covered verandah with a central room, and corner storage rooms called Pande ki Ovari and Sej ki Ovari on either side. Pande ki Ovari was used to store jewellery, and Sej ki Ovari for storing the rulers' clothes. On the inside, the temple type stone columns supporting stone brackets show intricate carving.

Located below the Nika ki Chopad, the Salehkhana comprises of a series of vaulted spaces with smaller vaulted rooms at the ends serving as storage spaces. It was initially conceived as the *Mardana* of Rai Angan block in the 16th century and later used for the storage of arms and ammunition. Presently, it is the first gallery one encounters while visiting the museum and has displays of arms and weapons. The vaulted architectural structure of the Salehkhana is inspired from the earlier palaces of Chittorgarh and Kumbhalgarh as well as the more contemporary ones built at Gogunda and Moti Magri. The form has a rugged, cave like appearance with heavy stone walls, arcuated ceiling and minimal ornamentation. The exterior has the typical projected opening in the centre. The initial *gokhda* (projected window) that resembled its precedents in style was closed in the 17th century with a small central cusped arch. The original temple type columns of the opening are still visible through the plaster.

The idol of Dhuni Mata presiding within Nauchowki Mahal

A Coronation ceremony in Rai Angan, The City Palace, Udaipur, 1930, Acc. No: 2008.05.0056 i

Historic precedents in Kumbhalgarh, Kumbha Palace

Kumbha Palace, Chittorgarh. Acc. No: 2009.10.0096-00005

Based on the axial layout of Sabha Shiromani and Amar Mahal and Zenana Mahal along the primary axis of Rai Angan, it is evident that these spaces were conceived around the same time. Amar Mahal and Zenana Mahal blocks are on the same axis as Rai Angan, located on a lower level to the south. They also have similar vaulted substructure and utilise the natural topography in the same manner as the Salehkhana block. The Sabha was originally a simple colonnaded structure with no enclosure such as the one found in Chittorgarh. The *Chittor-Udaipur Paatnaama* clearly describes about the ten palace structures constructed by Maharana Udai Singh II below the Machla Magra including the Zenana and the Mardana sections. It is possible that these were partially destroyed during the times of turmoil between 1572 AD and 1605 AD when the royal family of Mewar was based in Gogunda, Chawand, and Udaipur was under the Mughals for a brief span. Since 1559 AD, the Sabha Shiromani has been accessed through the Mardana Deodhi, which is the main entrance gate facing Manek Chowk. There have been several stylistic changes and additions to the gateway in the 18th and 20th century as can be deduced from historic paintings and descriptions. Essentially, the original entrance would have been a straight flight of steps with a primary gateway—a stone lintel opening with ornamental cusps on either side. This would lead into a smaller second opening, which would enter into the Sabha. Hence, the inner core of the palace during Maharana Udai Singh II's reign would have extended from the Rai Angan and the Salehkhana to the Kothar on one end and portions of Bhandar Chowk and Lakshmi Chowk on the other.

Sabha Shiromani ka Darikhana

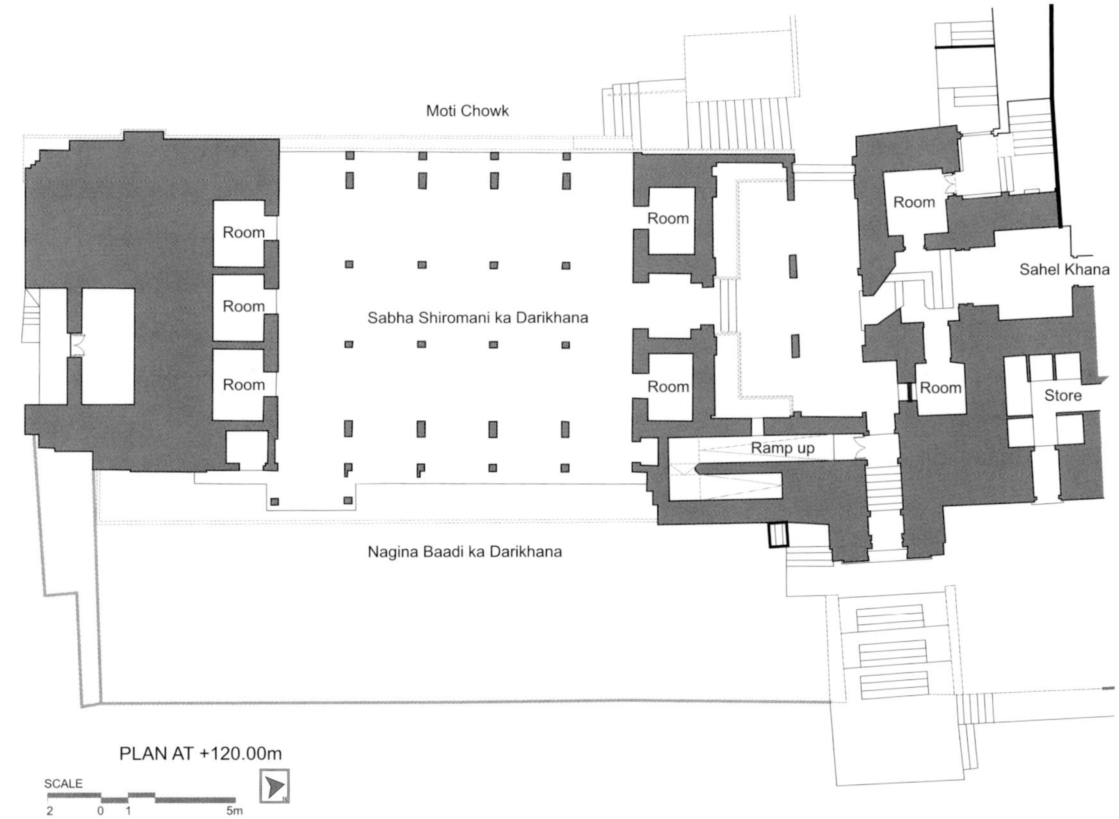

Left Above: Plan of Sabha Shiromani

Below: Reconstructed section through Rai Angan and Manek Chowk showing the original form of palace buildings

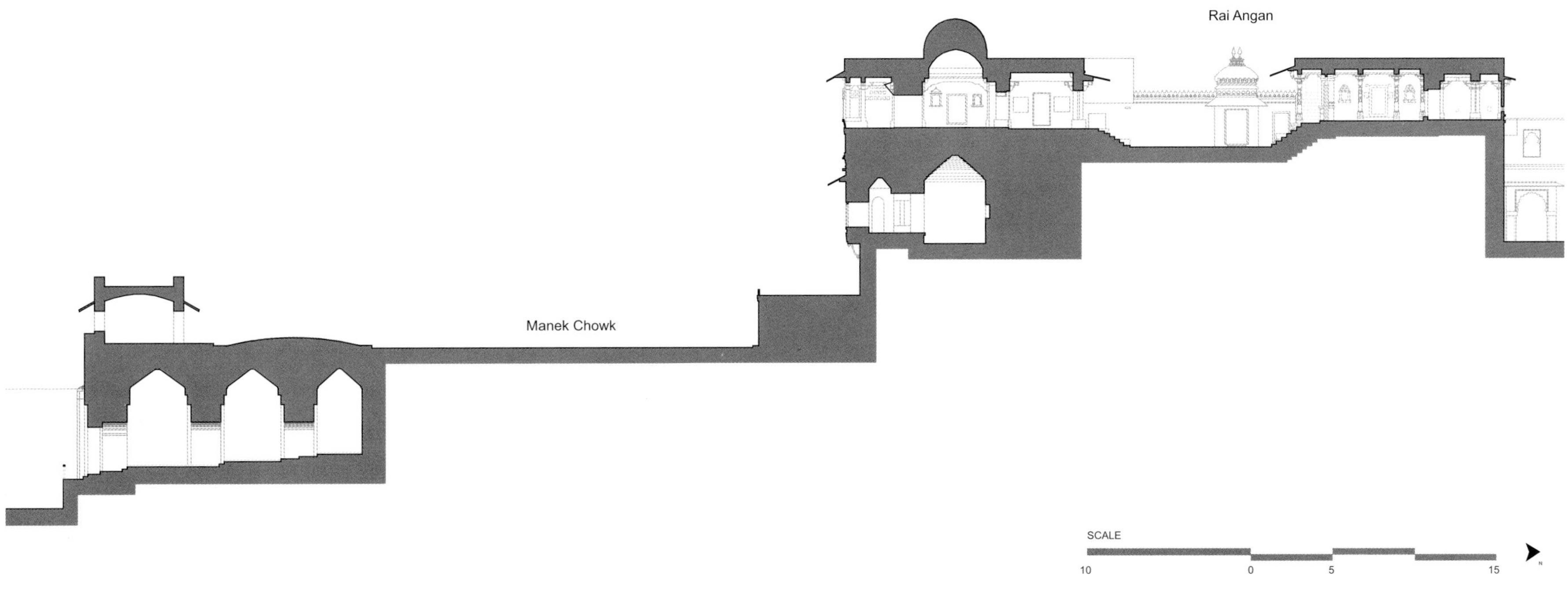

Amar Mahal as Rawala (Zenana)

Initially, the Kothar—an area located toward the north of the City Palace, was a part of the old *rawala* or *zenana,* which was planned during the reign of Maharana Udai Singh II. During the reign of his successor, Maharana Amar Singh I, the surrounding chambers became the central store of the palace and were used for storing food grains and other items, which were distributed to different sections of the palace. Food items for horses and elephants were also stored here. Many 18th century paintings depict servants carrying sacks of grains across the courtyard or engaged in other activities such as separating different types of food grains, presumably for the purpose of distribution.

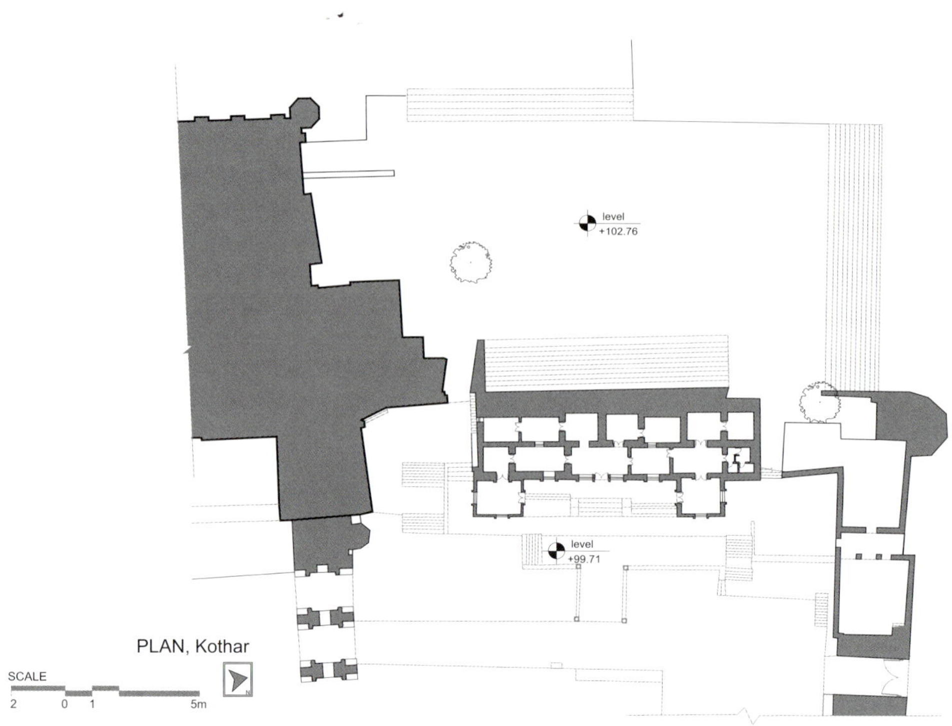

Top: Plan for Kothar which served as the original Zenana in the City Palace

Left: View of Bhandar Chowk, Amar Mahal

Above: Vaulted roof forms within Amar Mahal

The Bhandar Chowk, an open courtyard located west of Amar Mahal, was the second ladies' courtyard of the palace, built in the 17th century during the reign of Maharana Amar Singh. Initially the courtyard was used for the royal wedding rituals and subsequently used for various religious rituals, including the sacrificial offering of goats to the local deity Ban Mata in the early 19th century. The Amar Mahal itself was constructed as a grandiose structure, to shift the *rawala* to the south of the main palace. In the 18th century this palace became a treasury. The interior and exterior of Amar Mahal is built in white marble, with vaulted and corbelled stone ceilings, stone carved temple type columns, *gokhdas* with inclined parapets and intricately carved niches. The structure is made in ashlar block masonry of marble similar in shape and size to contemporary structures such as the Nauchowki in the City Palace and the original structure of Damdama, which later became the famous Jagmandir in the Lake Pichola.

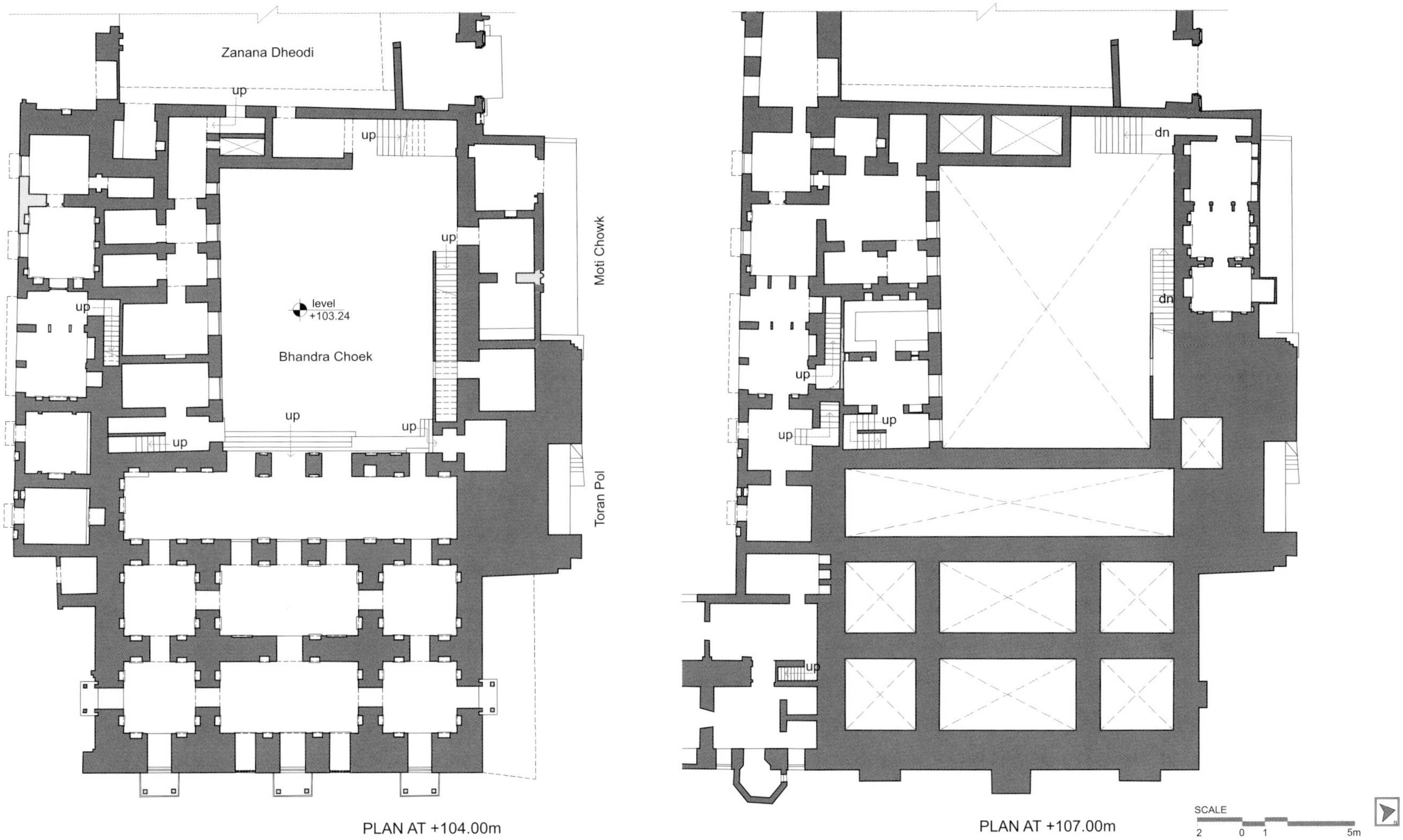

Plans of Bhandar Chowk, Amar Mahal

Peripheral Spaces

Towards the outer periphery of the main palace, which comprised of Rai Angan, Bhandar Chowk, portions of Lakshmi Chowk and Kothar were other gateways and structures. At the location of Suraj Pol, there most likely was a gate that was destroyed during the Mughal siege, when the palace was abandoned for a short period. This structure predated Badi Pol, situated to the north end of the palace, which was constructed in the 17th century. A vaulted sub-structure, which presently forms the foundation of Manek Chowk, leading from the site of this older gateway can also be dated to 1559 AD, contemporary to Salehkhana block. Its structural and spatial similarity to the Salehkhana block indicated that it is a part of the earliest historic fabric of the palace. These cells have been originally carved out on the edge of the hill marking the external boundary of the palace. This subterraneous space used to be a store in times of siege, for horse and elephant fodder, and grain for humans. Being partially underground, with only one facet available for ventilation and light, the space was dark and humid. The space formerly used as a storehouse was walled up for more than a century as Mewar had discontinued the sieges. The rudimentary structure of the space consists of three long parallel vaults, interspersed by cross passages. The space, although devoid of any decoration was powerful and dramatic in its dimensions. The vaults are over 20 feet high, and the interspersed walls are 10 feet thick.

The Badi Pol, literally the big or main gate, was constructed by Maharana Amar Singh I in the early 17th century, and continues to serve as the main northern entrance point to the City Palace. The original inscription in Arabic, which was written by a *qazi*, still exists on the gate, dating it to 1615 AD. A small temple of Annapoorna Mata was also made by Maharana Amar Singh I and the *Shilalekh* (inscription in foundation stone) in this temple, mentions that the *Prathishthan* or the foundation ceremony of the Badi Pol was during the reign of Maharana Amar Singh I. The adjoining areas served as spaces for guards. The construction techniques used in the Badi Pol included the use of the corbelled arch with carved stone brackets, similar to the types used in entrances of earlier forts of Kumbhalgarh and Chittorgarh. This

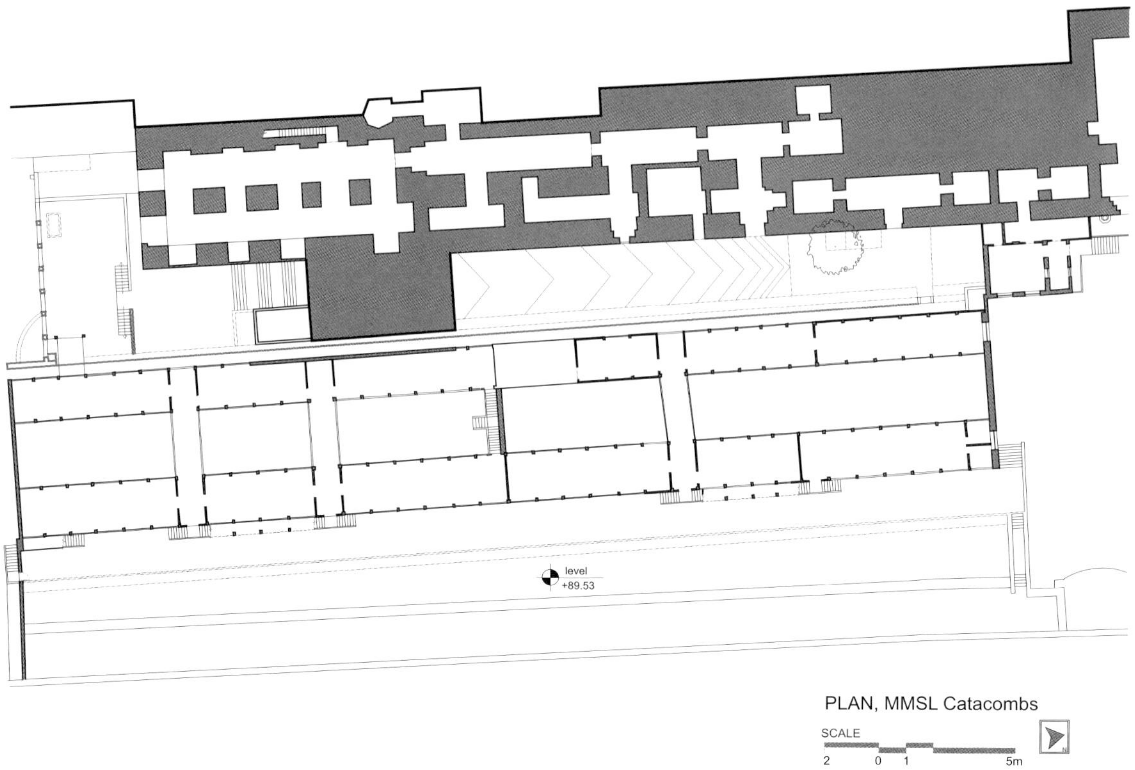

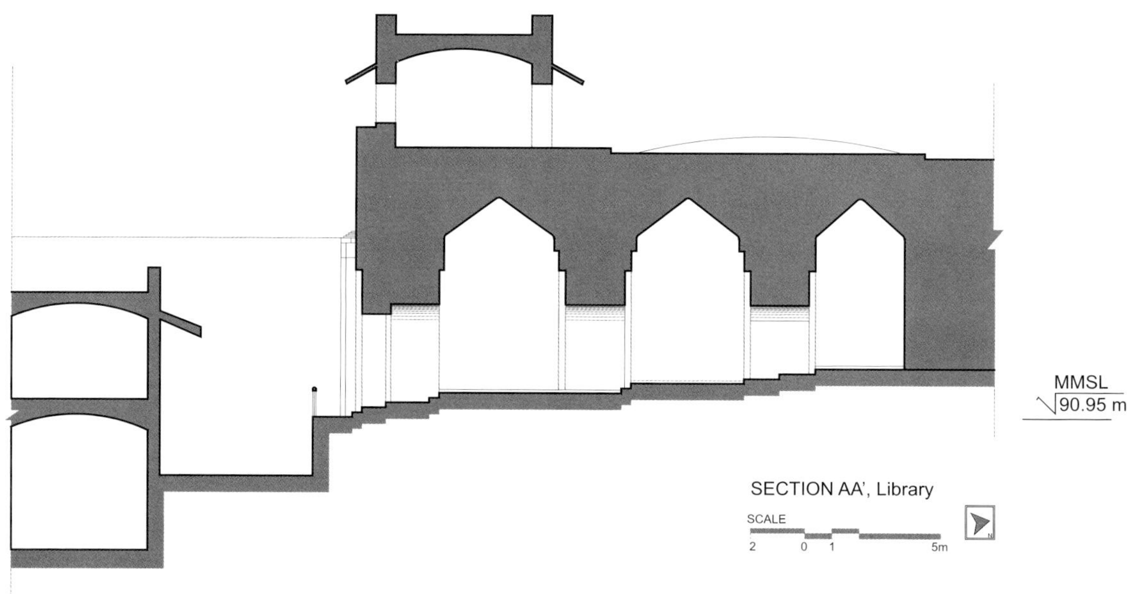

Above: Plan and section of the catacombs area which presently forms the foundation for Manek Chowk

gate shows the persistence of style and continuity of architectural techniques from 14th century to early 17th century in Mewar. The Badi Pol leads into a courtyard that gradually rises with the topography of the hill, and is located beyond the *rawala* or the Kothar area. This courtyard contains the location of Bhairav, the spot marked by Maharana Udai Singh II in the once dense forest and is till date associated with the founding of Udaipur city. The eastern edge of the court was rough, uneven and at a lower ground level with a gate called the Paiga ki Pol leading to the stables area.

The distinctive style of this period was characterised by the use of heavy masonry with thick walls, vaulted substructures and roofs, and trabeated construction with carved temple type stone columns and beams inspired by previous Mewar precedents of the Kumbha Mahals at Kumbhalgarh and Chittorgarh. These palace structures were often capped with round domes with a lotus finial. Other features were stone *chajjas* with lipping, inclined stone parapet in openings resting on carved stone brackets.

Top: View of Badi Pol, with Tripoliya Gate in the background, The City Palace, Udaipur, 1865-1890 CE, Acc. No: 2008.06.0108

Above: View of Badi Pol today

View of Jagmandir Island Palace, Udaipur, 1895-1905 CE
Acc. No: 2009.10.0139-00004

Expansion of the Palace

Mewar-Mughal Early Phase

The period extending from 1620 to 1698 AD saw the continuing expansion of the City Palace and the gradual incorporation of Mughal architectural influences. The architectural planning, form and details are representative of the cordial relationship established between the rulers of Mewar and the Mughals, and show an interesting amalgamation of the earlier Mewar styles with newly gathered Mughal ideas of architecture. At the same time, there was lingering resistance to foreign styles and structures that were purely characteristic of the Mewar style, such as the *torans* near the Badi Pol, continued to be built. During this phase, the courtyards and their palaces were generally planned on a much larger public scale, for instance, Manek Chowk, Lakshmi Chowk in Zenana Mahal, and Moti Chowk which were all considerably larger than the pre- existing Rai Angan and Bhandar Chowk. However, within the planning of these courts, there is little evidence of a purely geometrical layout in place, and minimal vegetation, which was quite disparate from the Mughal approach to open spaces and gardens. The architectural form of palace structures in this phase, such as the Karan Mahal, first floor spaces of the Rai Angan- namely the Chandra Mahal and Lakhu Gokhda, Dilkhushal Mahal and interventions in Sabha Shiromani and Zenana Mahal, show increasing Mughal exchange. The spatial quality in this phase retained the low height enclosed ambience by the closure of earlier *jharokhas*, and further division of space by smaller height columns, seen in Zenana Mahal and Sabha Shiromani block. This phase also marks the introduction of cusped arches in the palace, which further evolved in the later phases. Prior to this, the arch in Mewar architecture was only used as a structural element.

The Alliance and New Constructions

In 1620 AD, Maharana Amar Singh I was succeeded by his son, Karan Singh (r. 1620–1628 AD). Maharana Karan Singh maintained the friendly relations with Emperor Jehangir that had been established by his father. These administrative decisions ensured that peace prevailed in the state, and the capital could be expanded and fortified. The return of peace also provided a fresh impetus to construction and this period saw the erection of several buildings, including palaces. Manek Chowk—the palace grounds in front of the Mardana Mahal was one of the first spaces constructed by Karan Singh in 1620 AD. Additions to the palace structures of the Rai Angan were also undertaken. One of the central areas of the City Palace, Mor Chowk was built as a new *durbar* area. Apart from the ambitious expansion of the palace structures, he also undertook construction of the water ditches, which received storm water and overflow from Lake Pichola and transferred it to Udai Sagar, where the water was used for irrigation. The Champa Bagh was also constructed within the city. One of the most historically significant events of Maharana Karan Singh's reign was the establishing of an honorary kinship with the Mughal Prince Khurram. Prince Khurram was provided asylum in Mewar for an extended period, where Karan Singh compounded the cordiality of his hospitality by an exchange of turbans with Prince Khurram. Such an exchange of headgear had long been a recognised token in India, proclaiming that henceforth two would remain bound by cords of friendship and fraternity. Prince Khurram spent several months at Udaipur residing in the pavilion palace in Lake Pichola now known as Jagmandir, before leaving Mewar for the Deccan. The garden of Jagmandir, the nearby island palace was started by Maharana Karan Singh and completed by Maharana Jagat Singh I. It is a fine blend of the sacred grove concept of Hindu landscapes integrated with the two dimensional geometrical pattern of the Mughal landscapes.

After succeeding his father Maharana Karan Singh, Maharana Jagat Singh I (r. 1628-1652 AD) attempted to repair Chittorgarh, in contravention of the 1615 Mewar-Mughal treaty to severely undermine the peaceful relations that had been established by his grandfather and father. An open conflict was avoided only through the mediation of the Emperor's eldest son, Prince Dara and for the next few years the political situation in Udaipur was more or less stable. Maharana Jagat Singh was recognised as a great patron of learning and the arts. His reign saw the construction of Udaipur's famous Jagdish, or Jagannath Rai temple, as well as completion of work on Jagmandir. Jagat Singh also held a number of *Tula-daan* ceremonies – in which he was weighed in gold and silver and the amount given away in charity to *brahmins* and the needy. On previous occasions, it was silver that was given away, but during 1648-52 AD gold was distributed at the *Tula-daan* ceremonies. This ceremony was repeated eight times during Jagat Singh's reign, and a series of *torans* were constructed to commemorate each event. These were built on the eastern wall of the City Palace adjacent to the Badi Pol. He also undertook construction of the Kanwarpada ka Mahal to the south of the palace structures.

Maharana Karan Singh
AD 1620 - 1628

Maharana Jagat Singh I
AD 1628 - 1652

Maharana Raj Singh I
AD 1653 - 1680

Maharana Jai Singh
AD 1680 - 1698

Under the patronage of Maharana Jagat Singh, illustration of several religious books and manuscripts was undertaken and court scenes and activities were visually documented. The Mewar style of painting, which was characterised by a dazzling use of colour, stylised trees and depiction of natural life reached a stylistic pinnacle. Painters such as Sahib-ud-din were patronised, and an extensive series of illustrations including the *Raga-mala* were prepared during this time.

The throne passed to Raj Singh (r.1652-1680 AD), after the death of Maharana Jagat Singh in 1652 AD. Like his predecessors, Maharana Raj Singh too undertook the task of refortifying Chittorgarh contrary to the treaty with the Mughals, which Mewar had accepted in 1615 AD. This would have led to a direct confrontation, which was only avoided through a series of negotiations between the Maharana and the Mughal Emperor Shah Jahan. Maharana Raj Singh sent several conciliatory envoys to Shah Jahan and dissuaded him from attacking Chittor. However, these negotiations were only partially successful, with the end result that the demolition of the new fortifications at Chittor was carried out unhindered. As a result of the deteriorating relations between Mewar and the Mughals, Maharana Raj Singh refrained from supporting Aurangzeb in the war for succession.

As a result of these and other factors - including that of emphasising Imperial sovereignty, Aurangzeb launched an offensive against Raj Singh in 1679 AD. The Mewar administration shifted to the hilly safety of the Bhomat plateau, and encouraged the citizens to leave Udaipur, as well as the hamlets and villages that fell on the route of the Mughal army. However this protracted confrontation proved to be disastrous for both sides and subsequently both sides realised that negotiating peace was the only viable solution to the situation in Mewar. While negotiations were still continuing, Raj Singh breathed his last at Oda, near Kumbhalgarh, in the late autumn of 1680 AD.

Despite the political turmoil, Maharana Raj Singh's reign saw an increase in the overall prosperity of Mewar. An able administrator and military commander he is credited with strengthening, both, the administrative machinery and army of

TOP: View of the Jagmandir Island Palace, Udaipur

ABOVE: View of the Jagdish Temple, Udaipur, 1930-1940 CE, Acc. No: 2008.07.0159

Mewar. Ranchod Bhatt's Raj Prashasti, a Sanskrit eulogy *('prashasti')* is one of the best known works dating to Raj Singh's reign. Another of Bhatt's famous works is the Sanskrit text called *'Amar Kavya'*, which details the rulers of Mewar from early times up to the reign of Raj Singh. Other Sanskrit texts of note include the *'Raj Ratnakar'* by the poet Sada Shiva, Jagannath Paliwal's *'Rajabhishek-Paddhati'*, on the coronation of Maharana Raj Singh and Lal Bhatt's *'Raj Singh Prabhao Varman'*, eulogising Raj Singh's reign. Mukan Kshotari's *'Raj Singhasan'* also dates to this period. Raj Singh patronised music also, and in the field of architecture, ordered the construction of many structures—ranging from palaces to lakes, water reservoirs and water-side pavilions, dams and tanks, most significantly the Rajsamand. He also encouraged the construction of temples (including the temple of Amba Mata) and gardens. However, despite his enthusiasm for the arts, no significant contribution to the City Palace may be attributed to him.

Maharana Raj Singh was succeeded by his son, Jai Singh (r. 1680–1698 AD). Terms for an end to the Mughal-Mewar confrontation were awaiting finalisation at this time. Realising that peace with Aurangzeb was even more imperative now, Jai Singh concluded an alliance with Emperor Aurangzeb. Respite from the constant confrontation that had plagued his father's reign, meant that Maharana Jai Singh could focus on the task of consolidating the capital city. One of his crowning engineering achievements was the construction of the Jaisamand reservoir. He also enlarged the Lake Pichola's extents and created an effective fresh water network. However, like his father before him he did not undertake any major construction activity within the City Palace itself.

Top: View of Lake Rajsamand and Nav Chowki Mahal, Kankroli, 1865-1890 CE, Acc. No: 2008.06.0147

Above: View of Jagniwas (Now Lake Palace Hotel), Udaipur, 1950-1955 CE, Acc. No: 2009.09.0229-00002

View of Chand Pol bridge on Lake Pichola from Lake Swarup Sagar, 1895-1905 CE, Acc. No: 2009.10.0139-00019

Expansion of the Open Spaces

This phase is characterised by significant expansion of the palace open spaces after an extensive exercise of renovation and rebuilding. Most of the construction activity can be attributed to the reign of Maharana Karan Singh. His was the first formal coronation ceremony that was held in the Rai Angan, a ritual that was continued for centuries of subsequent rulers. Despite the debate which surrounds the actual dates of construction of the Zenana section or Amar Mahal, the actual delineation of sections through the creation of the Zenana Deodhi and the Ganesh Deodhi was redefined by him. Both entrance points marked the distinct parts of the palace; the newly constructed Zenana and the expanding Mardana. This phase also set the trend for the various activities, festivals and processions which would be held in different spaces, thus delineating specific uses to the courtyards and the built structures.

Left: The serpentine brackets that characterise the architecture vocabulary of this phase

Below: Additions and modifications to the skyline in the second phase of evolution

Facing Page: Expansion of the palace during its second phase of development

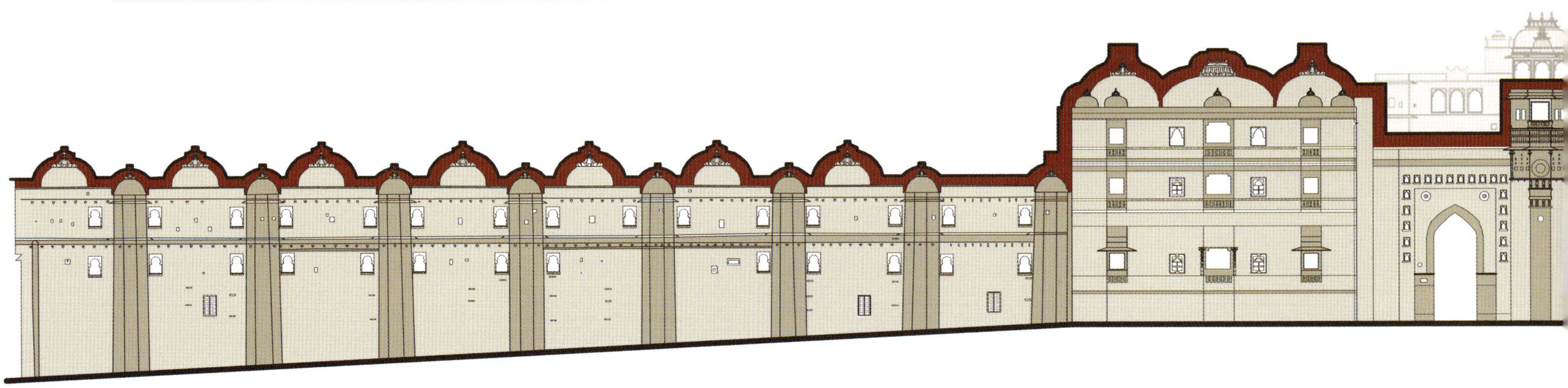

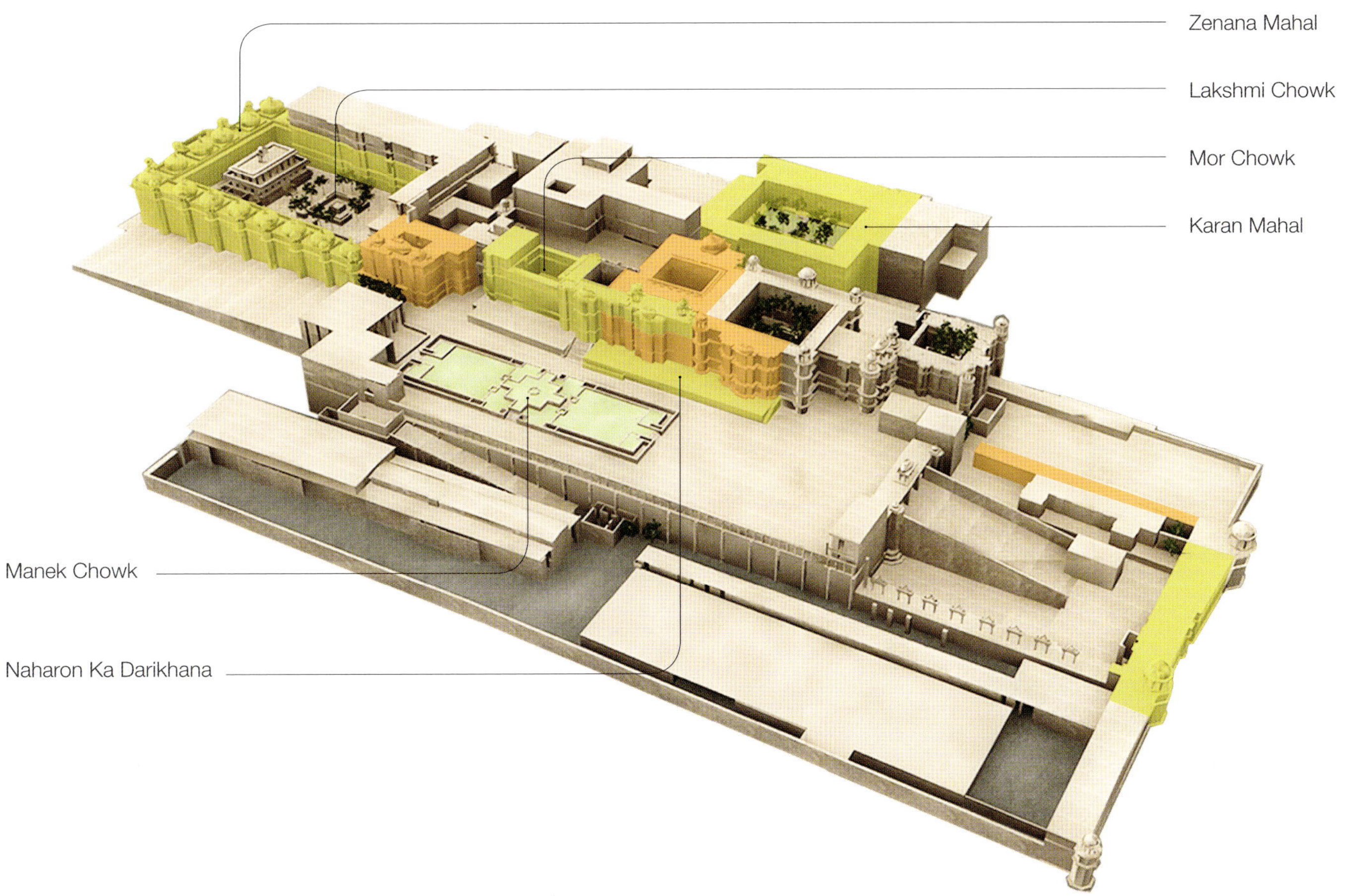

Zenana Mahal
Lakshmi Chowk
Mor Chowk
Karan Mahal
Manek Chowk
Naharon Ka Darikhana

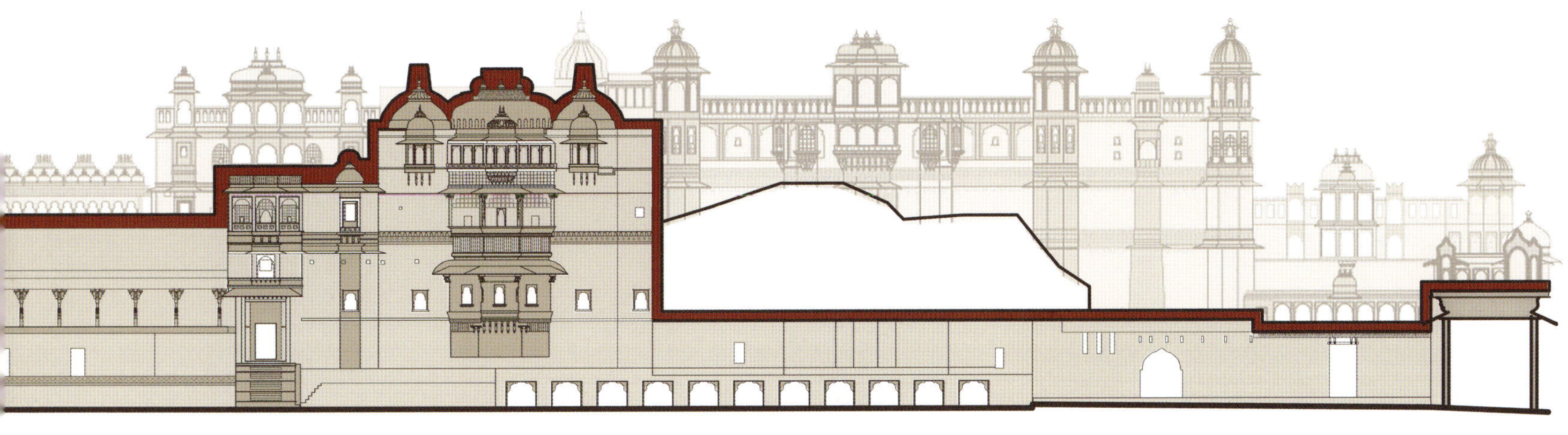

Additions to Rai Angan (Mardana)

The first elements that emerged from the Mewar Mughal synthesis can be observed in the insertion of cusped brackets in the earlier straight opening so as to give the appearance of a cusped arch opening. Examples of this can be seen in the entrance to Salehkhana and Sabha Shiromani. Similar elements were used in the additions to Rai Angan structures, such as Rang Mahal and Chandra Mahal which were added above Nauchowki and Dilkhushal Mahal which was built over the Nika ki Chopad. Chandra Mahal was created by Maharana Karan Singh as a royal leisure space. Early depictions of this space show that celebrations of festivals such as *Holi* and dance performances were regular events.

The central space contains a square shaped water reservoir, which may have been used during *Holi*. The steps leading from the Nauchowki open into a terrace that leads to Rang Mahal on the north and the Lakhu Gokhda on the south. The Lakhu Gokhda is a covered projecting balcony with an elaborate marble seat used by Maharana Karan Singh. The seat rests on a platform that overlooks the terrace leading to the Rang Mahal. The marble columns that support this platform have been crowned with cusped brackets, which is characteristic of the architectural style favoured by the Maharana. The balcony itself has delicately carved *jaalis* in different geometrical patterns, which are a clear Mughal influence. Directly above the Rang Mahal, is the Kacheri Mahal constructed in the same phase, with the similar stylistic influences. The exterior east façade shows the stone chajjas and square openings typical to that period. The Dilkhushal Mahal was built above the Nika ki Chopad, along with the adjoining rooms, the Chitram ki Burj and the Kanch ki Burj connected through a semi-covered verandah overlooking the Rai Angan. This space was ostensibly used for religious ceremonies, as evident from 18th century paintings. The Kanch ki Burj, though constructed during the reign of Maharana Karan Singh, was embellished with its intricate mirror work only during the reign of Maharana Shambhu Singh many decades later. The Chitram ki Burj was a space toward the southern side of the Kanch ki Burj and symmetrical to it with the north door opening into the Dilkhushal Mahal and the south one opening into the semi-covered area of the Sat Tanka. The room was built in the early 17th century. This was covered with murals and paintings in the early 17th century during the reign of Maharana Sangram Singh. The *Rawal Ranaji ri Baat* mentions the welcome of the Mughal Emperor Shahjahan and his stay in the Kacheri Mahal and Nauchowki area.

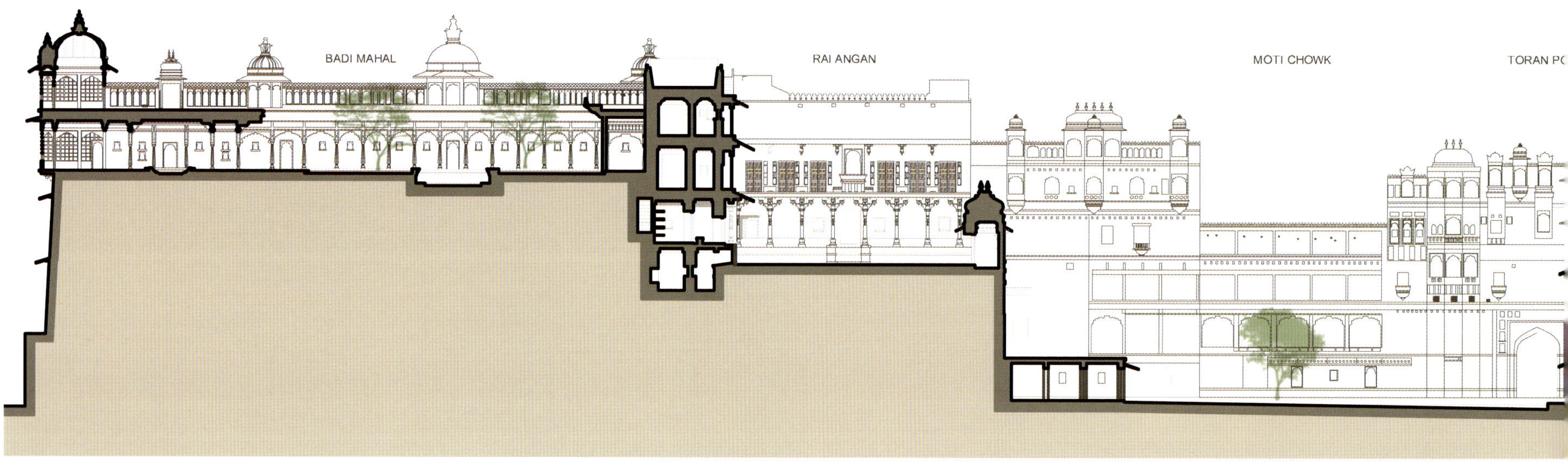

Above: The Lakhu Gokhda used by Maharana Karan Singh
Below: Longitudinal section through the City Palace

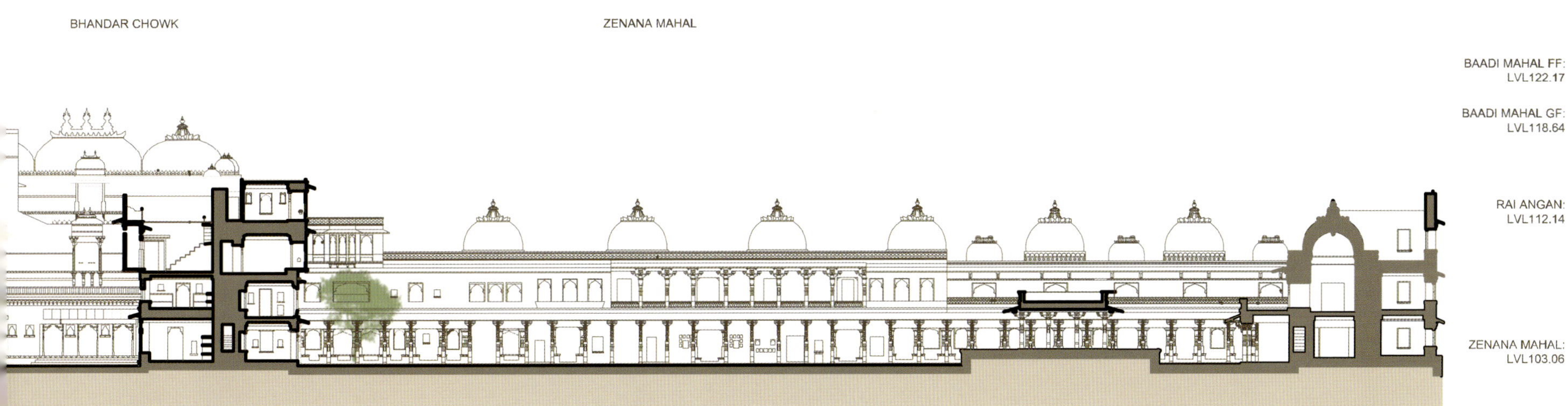

Moti Chowk and Ganesh Chowk

One of the most significant additions to the palace by Maharana Karan Singh was the addition of Moti Chowk between the pre-existing Rai Angan and the Bhandar Chowk area. This *chowk* formed the transition space between the Mardana and the Zenana, through the addition of smaller *chowk,* such as Ganesh Chowk and was the centre-point of most royal visits and processions. As the first inner courtyard of the Mardana, it holds great significance spatially. Functionally, this courtyard was very important; as it was here that the elephants and horses were prepared for royal visits and processions. It was used in conjunction with the elevated Ganesh Chowk to ride or dismount from the animals. Paintings of richly decorated horses and elephants still adorn some of the surrounding palace walls. It still functions as a space that both connects and separates the two main sections of the palace.

Satnavari Paiga, which literally means seven and nine bays, was also built during this phase. It consisted of two blocks at the northern and western edges of Moti Chowk, with the terrace of the north block forming Ganesh Chowk. Used to house the royal stables, the Paiga was a series of simple colonnaded spaces, the west block and part of the north block were later enclosed with walls. The monolithic stone columns and brackets were built in the basic temple style with minimal ornamentation.

The Chhota Darikhana was created as a colonnaded hall for meetings above the western wing of the Satnavari Paiga could be accessed from the Ganesh Chowk. It was conceived as a nine bay double aisle space with a high parapet on the terrace. The Kanwarpada ki Ori, which was later converted into the Khasa Rasoda, comprised of a small courtyard space

Maharana Bhupal Singh of Udaipur in procession from Zenana Deodhi, Moti Chowk, The City Palace, Udaipur, 1940-1950 CE, Acc. No: 2008.06.0440

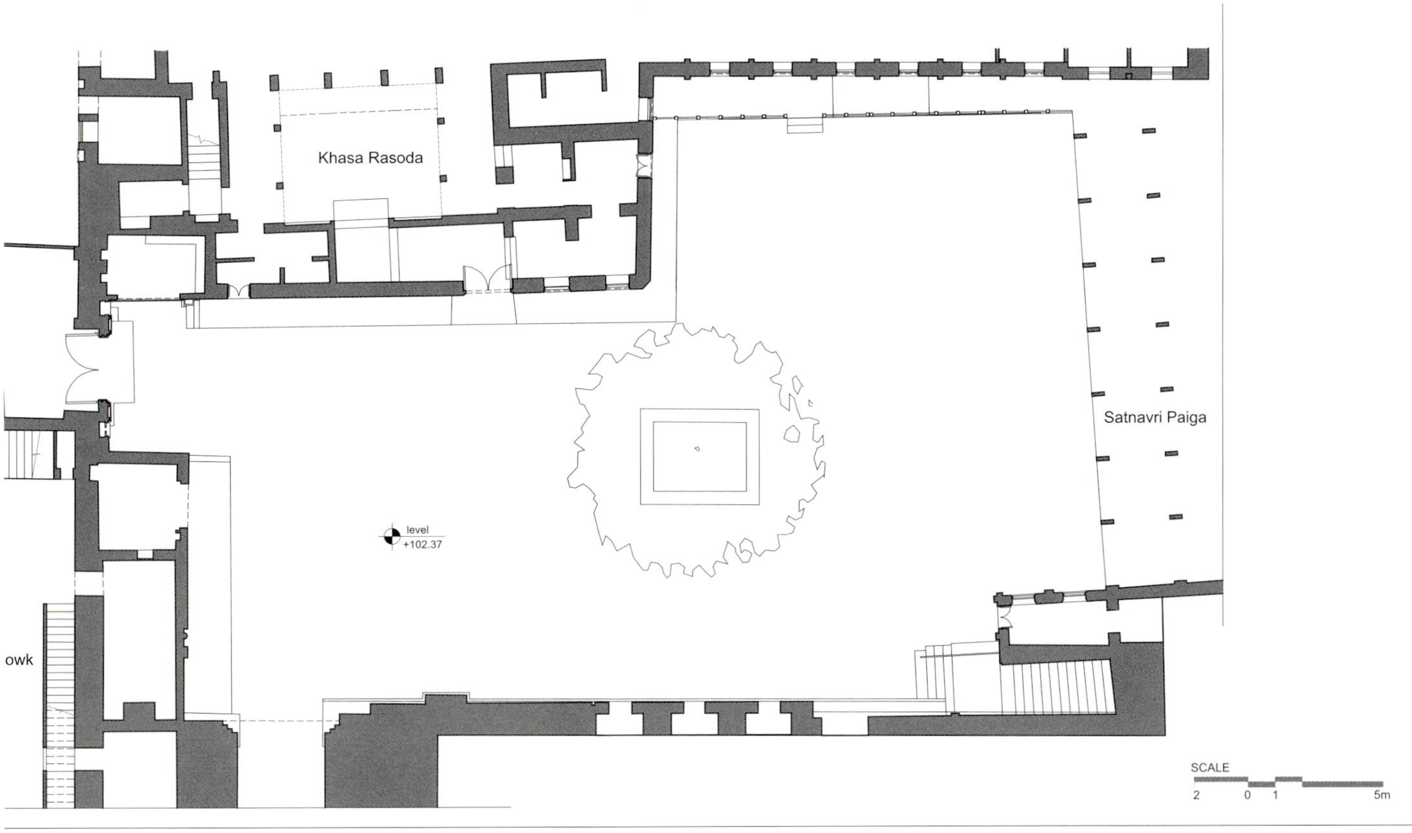

Top: Horses tethered in the Satnavri Paiga

Above: Plan of Moti Chowk

accessible from the Moti Chowk and surrounded by small rooms on three sides. There is little historic evidence to indicate its exact original form or use, but it was possibly a storage area for the prince.

Located on the terrace of the north block of Satnavri Paiga, Ganesh Chowk linked to major open spaces with the City Palace; Moti Chowk and Manek Chowk, since both spaces could be accessed through this space. It went on to connect these spaces to Rai Angan, through Ganesh Deodhi, effectively connecting all the significant spaces of the Mardana, through a single elevated terrace. Ganesh Deodhi formed the threshold to the most significant courtyard, Rai Angan. It was at this time, that the upper landing of the Ganesh Deodhi was also converted into an enclosed space with a *chhatri*, which opened into the Rai Angan. The oblong *chhatri* is stylistically characteristic of Maharana Karan Singh, and may be attributed to his reign as well.

Above: Ganesh Deodhi, Mardana Mahal, The City Palace, Udaipur. Acc. No: 2009.09.0107-00001

Right: Maharana Bhupal Singh of Udaipur riding an elephant on the Silver Howdah at Moti Chowk, The City Palace, Udaipur,1935 CE. Acc. No: 2008.06.0072 i

Additional chowks and darikhanas

South of Rai Angan and overlooking both Moti Chowk and the newly laid out Manek Chowk, Mor Chowk was originally built by Maharana Karan Singh as a Durbar area, with Manek Mahal to its north and Surya Chopad to its south. At this point, it was unadorned with the mirror mosaic and glass work, and used mostly as the *Deewan-i-Khas*. It was only in the 18th and 19th centuries that it would acquire the aesthetic splendour that makes it one of the most significant architectural spaces in the palace. Cultural performances, special *durbars* with nobles, where special guests were received marking historic turning points were all held in this *chowk*.

The Surya Chopad and Surya Gokhda was originally constructed by Maharana Udai Singh II, however in the extensive renovations undertaken by Maharana Karan Singh, this space was completely re-designed. Given that the members of the royal family would traditionally be referred to as *Suryavanshis,* or descendents of the Sun, the Surya Gokhda was and continues to be of great religious importance, as a space to pay homage to the Sun God. The Gokhda was essentially constructed as a small space with a projected opening facing east. It was entered through an enclosed bay - the Surya Chopad that has another *gokhda*, called Suk Niwas, opposite the Surya Gokhda on the west side. The projected sun window is right above the last bay of the Sabha Shiromani. The architectural style with the projected triple bays and small square openings on the side bays is typical of Maharana Karan Singh's reign. The central bay has a circular opening, and extensive modifications were made to the interior of this space during the 18th and 19th centuries.

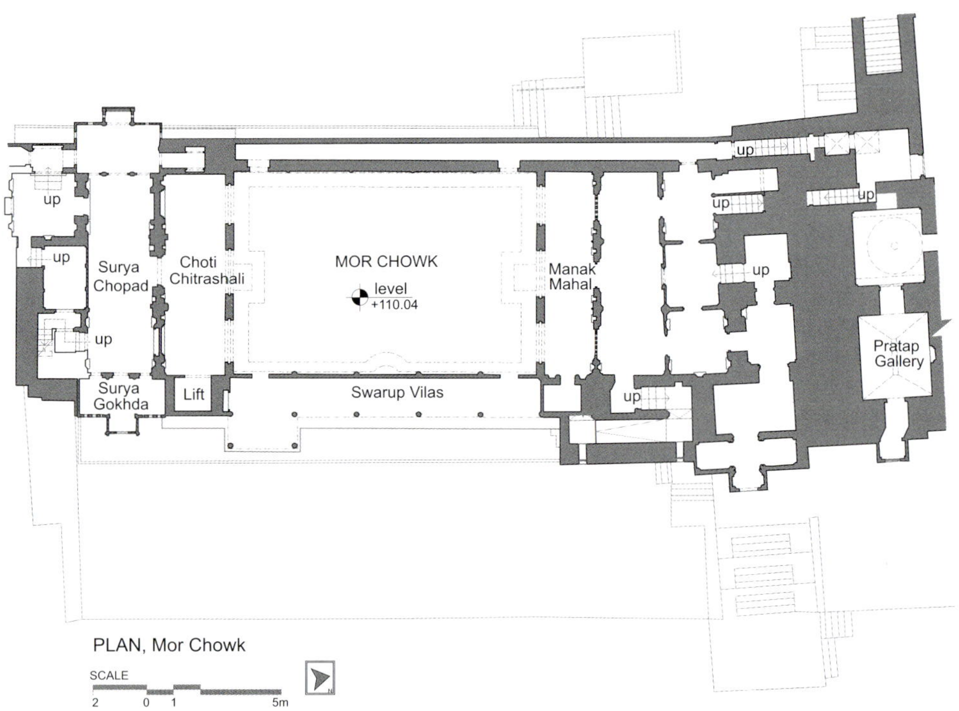

Plan of Mor Chowk

Surya Gokhda projecting onto Manek Chowk

Sabha Shiromani, built in the 16th century was renovated by Maharana Karan Singh, and the two northern entrance bays of the nine bays were used to create a columnar lobby space that stepped into the *darikhana.* The central space remained columnar and one last bay on either side was closed to create rooms. The lobby space from the Mardana Deodhi thus opened up into the Salehkhana on the north, the Sabha Shiromani on the south and into the open Ganesh Chowk in west. The lobby space initially had temple type stone columns supporting stone beams but the intervention by Maharana Karan Singh included additional walls and the insertion of cusped arches between the original columns.

Maharana Ari Singh II in durbar at night at Pitam Niwas terrace above the Surya Chopad, Udaipur
c.1765 by Bakhta
Source: National Gallery of Victoria, Melbourne.

Karan Mahal

One of the biggest palace structure of this period is the Karan Mahal earlier called the Rasode ka Mahal (dining palace). An 18th century painting from Chitram Ki Burj depicts this space which had a separate entrance called Rasode ka Pol and a horse stable outside. The palace itself is a beautiful colonnaded structure with cusped arches overlooking the Lake Pichola. Its foundation was laid by Prince Khurram. This palace was axially aligned to the west of Rai Angan block.

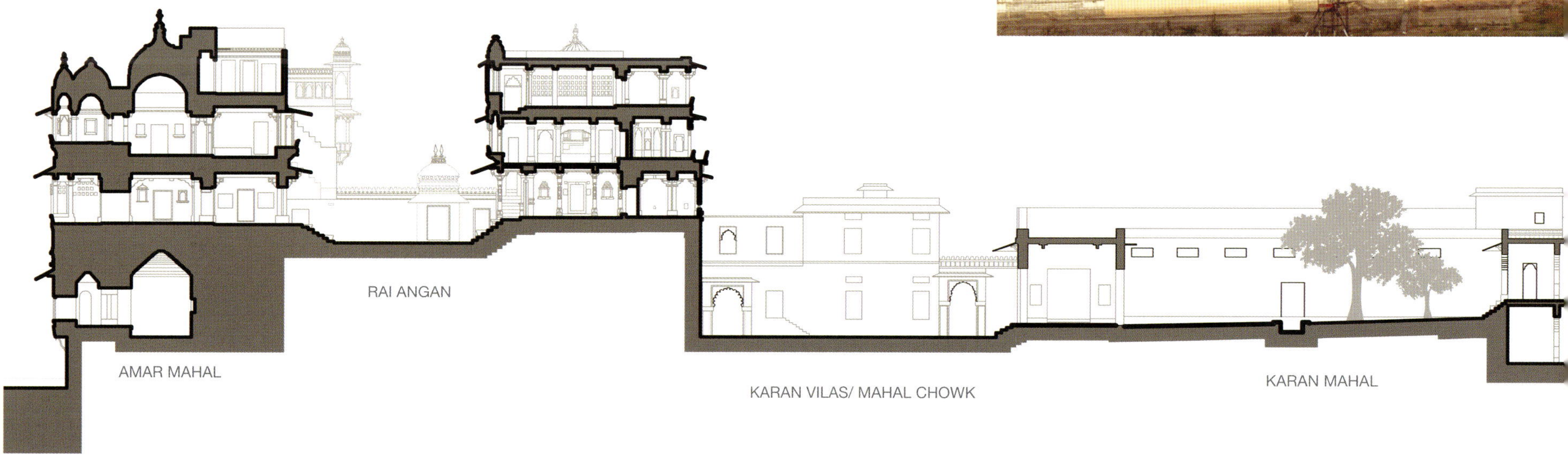

Top: Lake side view of Karan vilas

Above: Section through Rai Angan and Karan Vilas/ Mahal leading down to Lake Pichola

Zenana: Zenani Deodhi

The threshold to Zenana Mahal and Lakshmi Chowk, Zenani Deodhi is stylistically and proportionally similar to the Ganesh Deodhi. Both gateways are additions to Moti Chowk and Ganesh Chowk respectively, and effectively delineate the two portions of the City Palace. The Zenani Deodhi is defined with a wall and a cusped arched gateway. An earlier map of the 18th century shows the existing two gateways to the *zenana* section - the first smaller one called the Zenani Deodhi and the next one with an enclosed space and baffle wall entrance as the Badi Zenani Deodhi. These two gateways enclose a small court in between them which opens into the Bhandar Chowk on the east and the Pitamber Rai ji ka Chowk with a small temple on the west. The second gate which is the main Zenani Deodhi opening into Lakshmi Chowk has an installation of Lord Ganesha's idol in a niche from the early 17th century. The gates are similar to the main gates or *pols* though much smaller in scale. The inner main gate has a pointed arch with niches on each side, which is similar to the Toran Pol but reduced in size. The outer gate has a cusped arch entrance with a *chatri* that seems to be a later addition.

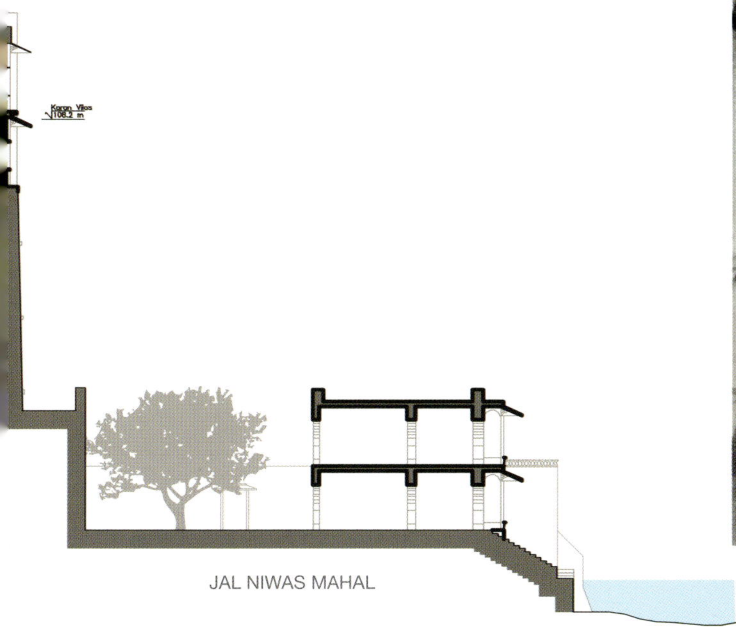

Nobles and Court Officials outside Zenana Deodhi, The City Palace, Udaipur, 1940-1950 CE, Acc. No: 2009.09.0087-00058

Lakshmi Chowk

Evidence suggests that portions of the *zenana* had already been constructed during the reign of Maharana Udai Singh II. Given the dearth of documentation and visual evidence for this portion of the City Palace, it is impossible to be certain, however, the actual configuration of Lakshmi Chowk as visible today is generally attributed to the reign of Maharana Karan Singh, owing to the stylistic similarities between the individual elements in Zenana Mahal to the other contemporaneous spaces in the City Palace. Lakshmi Chowk, which is the heart of the *zenana* is an enclosed inward looking large spacious court with royal apartments on four sides with solid external walls. The ground floor of the eastern wing has the *osara* or place of ceremony and celebration. The ladies of the court and their guests assembled here on auspicious and appropriate occasions for pleasure and gaiety. All the rituals concerning royal ladies were performed here, right from the weddings of princes and princesses, the recitation and chanting of hymns and *'yagna'* or offerings to the sacred fire. A painting on the palace walls around this courtyard shows the princess being carried in palanquin followed by lady attendants, indicating the common activities that took place here.

The courtyard has a few existing matured trees like mango, *neem* and *bael*. The fact that all these three types of trees have religious connotation is noteworthy, especially as *bael* is associated with Lord Shiva, the presiding deity of the royal family. A *tulsi bedi* is also present. *Tulsi* is symbolic of Lord Vishnu's protection and considered auspicious. Thus one can deduce that the court was self-contained in terms of its ritualistic requirements. This *chowk* provides access to the private palaces of the queens.

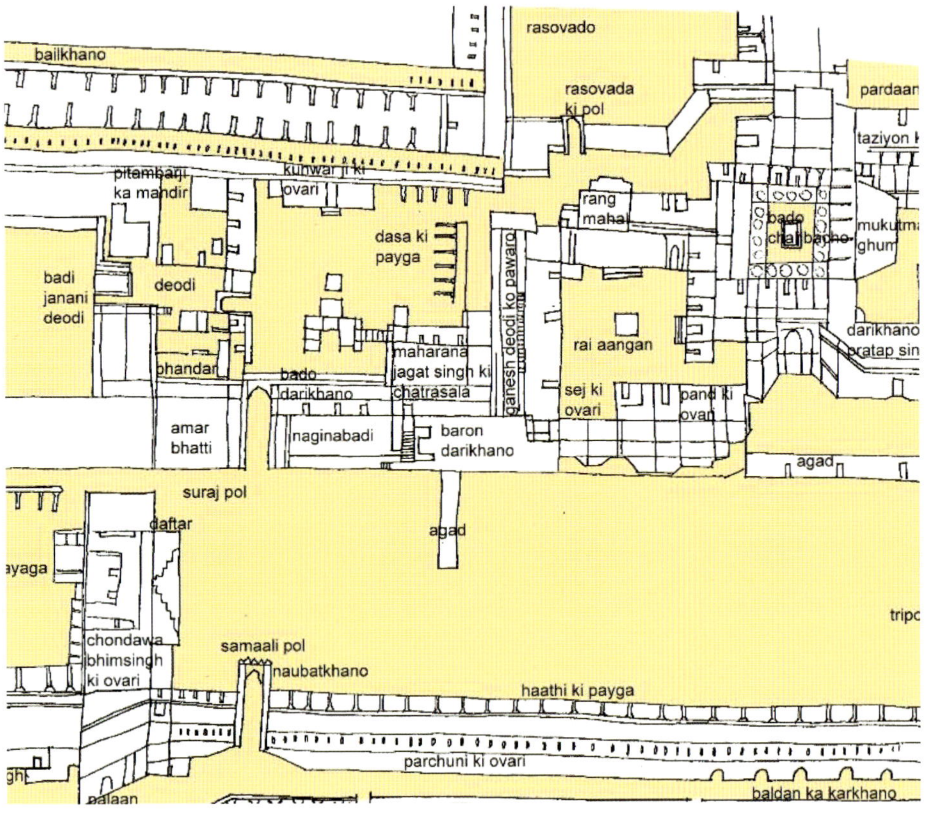

18th century recreated map showing Zenani Deodhi entry to Lakshmi Chowk

The northern wing of the *zenana* formed the linking block between the earlier Amar Mahal and the other three wings of the *zenana* which were possibly added later. The structure has low ceilings, multi-foliated arches and niches, and perforated windows so the ladies could look out without being seen from the outside. The eastern wing housed the main temple or *osara* in the centre portion, which is maintained as a religious space till today, and royal weddings are solemnised in the *osara*. Above the *osara* is the Jas Prakash Mahal, meant for ladies-in-waiting and wives of the nobles. The eastern wing is a double storeyed structure capped by a series of small round domes typical of the early Mewar style, with smaller oblong ones placed in between. This wing too has elements stylistically congruent with the northern wing. Paintings from the Chitram ki Burj show that the spaces in the *zenana* wings were subdivided, with separate units belongs to each queen. This wing is illustrative of the original form of all *zenana* wings as it has seen minimal later intervention. The west wing has small temples located within a colonnade at ground level. The west wing shows the maximum intervention during the 19th and 20th centuries.

The *zenana* or women's part of the *rawla* or *mahal* of a Maharani (her courtiers and ladies in waiting) had its own rituals and almost had a parallel 'court'. Except when the ruler or chief attended a gathering within the *zenana,* the functions and day-to-day life within the *zenana* palaces were presided over by the senior most among the queen-mothers; usually, though not always, this was the mother of the incumbent ruler or chief or sometimes by the senior most or most favoured queen. There existed a strict protocol for seating and so forth at the festivities, rituals and other functions held within the *zenana.* This phenomenon is reflected in the *zenana* architecture and its spatial hierarchies, leading from the large common courtyard to a series of smaller ones for certain individual queens or for specific rituals, spaces for certain trees or shrubs, and areas for public audiences and gatherings within the *zenana*. Religious rituals and preparations for these occupied numerous hours within the *zenana*. Activities associated with these included the cleaning and decoration of areas needed for ritual-use, preparation of clothes and vessels required for worship, for giving away to *brahmins, 'brahminis'* and *charans* in charity, making garlands, as also the refurbishing of the *zenana* inhabitants' clothes, applying *mehendi,* and the preparation of food by the various women servitors and their mistresses. In fact, the *zenana* was a universe of its own. When the ruler was to be present for a function within the *zenana,* there would be a different series of preparations, where the ruler would be the centre of all attention. Weddings and associated rituals involved a still lengthier preparation.

In the Udaipur City Palace, there was possibly an enclosure with a *zenana* which served as a swimming pool or place for *chebcha* near the base of the palace complex, along the lakeshore. This was accessed by a passage from a temple in the *zenana* area. There was also a tradition of the zenana ladies going for *'chebcha'* to the Jag Niwas (now the Lake Palace Hotel) on the occasion of Akha Teej or Akshay Tritya.

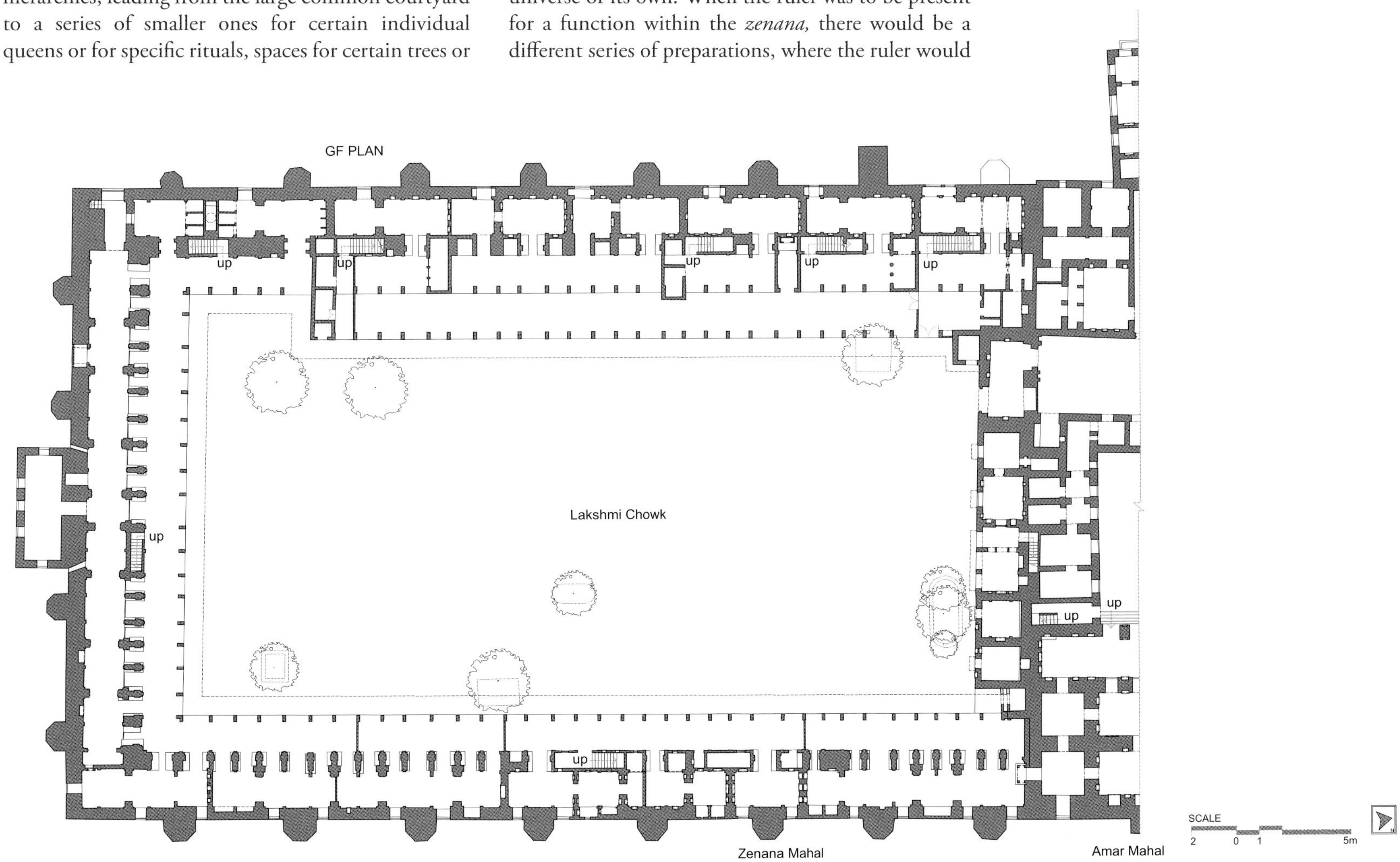

Plan of Lakshmi Chowk and Zenana Mahal

Peripheral Spaces
Manek Chowk

Constructed during the reign of Maharana Karan Singh, this became the largest courtyard of the City Palace, accessible from two sides through majestic gateways; Badi Pol to the north, constructed several years earlier and Suraj Pol (then known as the Samaali Pol) to the east. Toran Pol on the western side of this chowk led to the interior palace spaces and was constructed in the 17th century as well. Originally, this Pol was named as Suraj Pol, since the outer gate was Samaali Pol.

This Pol possibly predated the 17th century; the construction style of the gate with a pointed arch instead of the progressive cusped one as well as its niches and decorative features are similar to the Badi Pol and Amar Mahal. However, it is usually considered to have been completed during the reign of Maharana Karan Singh. Over the centuries, due to its association with the royal wedding rituals, its name changed to Toran Pol, the word *toran* translating into a temporary crown tied to the entrance gate. Opening into Moti Chowk, and connecting the public Manek Chowk with the Lakshmi Chowk, Toran Pol was especially significant for royal processions and weddings. Miniature paintings from the early 18th century show a dome on top of the gate, but this was possibly concealed later with high parapet walls.

The substructure for portions of Manek Chowk had already been constructed by Maharana Udai Singh II and the roofs of these underground vaulted chambers which were used as granaries, became a part of Manek Chowk. This *chowk* is the most public of spaces within the palace and has been the venue for celebration of festivals, outdoor activities and sports, functions, meetings and conferences for the rulers for centuries. Manek Chowk is depicted in most of the early paintings of the palace and shows a wide range of activities like wrestling, Holi celebration, elephant fights, processions etc. Historically, this was a plain paved surface and the gardens were developed only recently.

Torans added during Maharana Jagat Singh's I reign

The open *darikhanas* in the Manek Chowk exist as raised platforms against the eastern palace facade. These were used by the Mewar rulers during celebrations, rituals and festivals, as they came to serve as ideal locations for the ruler and the nobles to watch the performances/ events in Manek Chowk. The northern wing comprised of Naharon ka Darikahana which was the earliest structure in front of Salehkhana. Opposite these darikhanas on the east called the Paiga (the space to tie elephants). Further changes to Manek Chowk were made in the 17th, 18th and 19th centuries as the palace extents expanded and the palace evolved into a complex network of courts, royal residences and public spaces.

Between Manek Chowk and Badi Pol, a series of eight ornate Torans were built along the eastern wall, the construction of which was undertaken during the reign of Maharana Jagat Singh I. Each *toran* marks the *tuladaan* or ceremonial weighing of the rulers on their birthday in gold, silver and grains and the wealth was distributed to the Brahmins, after which the remainder was used to construct or maintain temples and reservoirs throughout the state. A few of the *torans* are attributed to Maharana Raj Singh I but these cannot be distinguished in terms of architectural style or materials from the ones constructed earlier. Each *toran* comprises of two intricately carved temple type stone columns with carved stone brackets and a stone lintel spanning the two columns. Two ornately carved brackets spring from the top of the columns and meet in the center of the span, forming a triangle on top of the lintel, giving the final form to each toran. The architecture is devoid of any Mughal influences, it is inspired by Hindu temple architecture entirely.

Top: Suraj Pol

Above: Maharana Bhupal Singh of Udaipur in procession from Toran Pol, The City Palace, Udaipur, 1940-1950 CE, Acc. No: 2009.10.0075-00009

Blending of Styles and Ideas

Mewar-Mughal Mature Phase

Even though the additions and alterations to the City Palace in this phase do not compare in scale to the earlier phase, some of the most architecturally outstanding structures and spaces within the palace were added during this period. This phase is characterised by a distinct stylistic change of architectural elements such as the dome and the arch, with the amalgamation of ideas with the pre-existing Mewar style. By the 18th century, the planning principles and underlying geometry of the Mughal architecture were fully integrated with Mewar style, especially in the City Palace. A classic example of this amalgamation is the Baadi Mahal, constructed on top of the highest point of the hill.

Political Turmoil and Palace Building

This phase covers the period of Maharana Amar Singh II's reign (r. 1698-1710 AD)to that of Maharana Hamir Singh II (r. 1773-1778 AD); a total of six rulers, but most of the contributions to the City Palace came from the first two, with minimal construction activity in the second half of the 18th century. The scale of the courtyards added in this phase was much smaller than in the previous phase. Despite this, the skyline of the palace was irrevocably changed, due to the addition of huge domes, and the Baadi Mahal and Chitrashali. A constantly changing political climate, marked by the declining power of the Mughals, the rise of the Kachchawahas and new confrontations with the Marathas, was possibly responsible for the diminishing construction activity in the later part of this phase.

During the early decades of this phase, new methods and technologies for propagation of horticulture and agriculture activities in the area and expansion of irrigation facilities to reach maximum land were put in place. A system of appointed caretakers for the gardens and plantations was devised. New vegetation and varieties of trees were planted in the 18th century like the wide-spreading tamarind, evergreen *khirni*, palmyra, cypress and cooling plantations that are still found within the City Palace.

Maharana Jai Singh was succeeded by Amar Singh II in 1698, amidst political turmoil in relation to the nobles and landholders. Thus, as one of his first royal campaigns, Maharana Amar Singh II (r. 1698-1710 AD) dispatched his forces against these states and enforced the re-establishment of Mewar's dominance over their affairs and the administrative units were re-organised. Gauging the rising power of the Kachchawaha Rajput ruler, Sawai Jai Singh II of Amber, Amar Singh II entered into a matrimonial alliance with him, through arranging the marriage of his daughter and an understanding with Ajit Singh of Marwar. While no significant additions to the capital city of Udaipur can be attributed to Maharana Amar Singh II, he made several expansions and alterations to the City Palace. The Baadi Mahal, which was the pinnacle of Mewar-Mughal amalgamation, is credited to him, and the two chatris on either side of the Badi Pol were also constructed during this period.

Maharana Sangram Singh II (r. 1710-1734 AD) succeeded his father on the throne, after a very short reign of 12 years by Maharana Amar Singh II. He profited greatly from the alliances formed by his father, especially in dealing with confrontations with the Imperial forces in the early years of his reign. Due to his close relationship with Sawai Jai Singh II, the political situation in Udaipur was more or less stable.

Maharana Amar Singh II
AD 1698 - 1710

Maharana Sangram Singh II
AD 1710 - 1734

Maharana Jagat Singh II
AD 1734 - 1751

Maharana Pratap Singh II
AD 1751 - 1754

Hence, Maharana Sangram Singh II was able to consolidate the capital, by adding new irrigation facilities to reach maximum land, and appointing caretakers for the gardens and plantations. He also added gardens and open spaces to the city, such as the Sahiliyon ki Badi. New seeds were distributed for plantations in Jag Mandir, Krishna Vilas, Naulakha Bagh and Champa Bagh. During the drought like conditions in Maharana Jagat Singh II's reign, he ordered the construction of Jag Niwas in the middle of Lake Pichola to provide livelihood to the local people. The dam on Lake Pichola may also be attributed to him. He also made additions to Jag Mandir and the Nahar Magra Mahal, Jagvilas and Shitla Mata Temple in Udaipur were completed during his reign. Maharana Sangram Singh's contribution to the City Palace was significant, through the addition of massive domes above the Kacheri Mahal and other spaces within the complex; he altered the skyline of the City Palace. Tripoliya, which was to become one of the architectural marvels of the palace was also conceived and built during his reign. Other structures such as Palki Khana, Badi Chitrashali, Chini Chitrashali , Vani Vilas and Kishan Vilas Sat Tanka were also built. Inspired by his brother-in-law Jai Singh, Sangram Singh also set up several astronomical instruments above Karan Mahal. The Hathi ka Agad and Hathnal ka Darikhana were smaller structures added to Manek Chowk.

The Mughal inspired water systems and fountains in Saheliyon ki Bari

Maharana Raj Singh II
AD 1754 - 1761

Maharana Ari Singh II
AD 1761 - 1773

Maharana Hamir Singh II
AD 1773 - 1778

Maharana Sangram Singh II was succeeded by Jagat Singh II (r. 1734-1751 AD), a time when Mewar had already begun facing interference from the Marathas, through the seizing of indemnities and intrusion into the internal court politics. The various rulers agreed upon cooperative measures to thwart the Maratha threat. Maharana Jagat Singh played a prominent part in these discussions which culminated in the signing of the 'Hurda Pact', the first time since the battle of Khanua in 1527 that a calculated formation of a Rajput confederacy came into being under the leadership of a Maharana of Mewar. Jagat Singh II's contribution to the capital's urban fabric or to the City Palace was minimal, with minor changes such as the addition of China tiles and Dutch Delft tiles in Badi Chitrashali and ornamentation near Surya Chopad.

When Maharana Jagat Singh II died in 1751, the throne was succeeded to by his estranged son Pratap Singh II (r. 1751-1754 AD). His short four year reign was fraught with Maratha incursions and infighting between several factions within his court. The sorry state of affairs in Mewar continued when Maharana Raj Singh II (r. 1754-1761 AD) succeeded his father at the age of 11. It is said that during Raj Singh's short reign the Marathas overran Mewar no less than seven times, reducing the state treasury to near ruin. The young ruler died without an heir, and the Mewar gaddi passed to his uncle Ari Singh II.

When Maharana Ari Singh II (r. 1761-1773 AD) succeeded to the throne after the untimely demise of his nephew, the political situation in Mewar was at its nadir, with the advancing forces of Holkar marching up to Udaipur and the complete alienation of nobles from the ruler. Given the poor economic situation and the constant lack of stability which marked the reign of Ari Singh, it is unsurprising that there is no record of construction at the City Palace during his reign. His brothers were responsible for the construction of Roop Ghat in the city as well as some smaller Jain temples. One useful addition during this period was a map of the City Palace which reflects the planning of the palace at that time.

Ari Singh's eldest son, the young Hamir Singh (r. 1773-177 AD) succeeded him. As the new Maharana was under-age, powers were exercised on his behalf by his mother, who took on the mantle of regent. Meanwhile, conditions in Mewar had continued to deteriorate. Over the next few decades, the Marathas, though hard-pressed by the increasing strength of the East India Company, both around the Maratha 'homelands', and across northern India, continued to raid and plunder Mewar and adjoining kingdoms of Rajasthan. Meanwhile, the rise of the East India Company soon introduced another factor that Mewar would need to reckon with.

Below: View of Chini Chitrashali exterior from Manek Chowk

Facing Page: Courtyard view of Chini Chitrashali showing Chinese tiles

Mewar Mughal Synthesis

This phase is characterised by the solidification of the various traditions and rituals associated with the various spaces within the City Palace. The Maharanas of Udaipur patronised local arts and craft and at the same time incorporated influences from Mughal art and architecture. Within the City Palace, the load bearing structural systems that had evolved from the previous phase used principles of the Karan Mahal with lower retaining wall encasing the original hill to locate the garden palace on the topmost ridge. This encasing as a fort type retaining wall exemplifies the palace-fortress form, typical of the Rajput architecture of this period. The Shiv Prasanna Amar Vilas (Baadi Mahal) imbibed Mughal ideas and design parameters, construction methods, engineering techniques and ways of maintenance. The concept of Mughal pleasure garden with plants, water and garden pavilions was improvised in the unique context of its natural terrain, where the garden itself was contained within an extensive colonnaded and covered verandah culminating in a typical Rajput pavilion overlooking the hills – thus the name Baadi Mahal (*baadi*-garden; *mahal*-palace).

LEFT: Section through the Mukut Mandir over Baadi Mahal

BELOW: Additions and alterations to the City Palace skyline in the third phase

FACING PAGE: Expansion of the City Palace in the third phase of its evolution

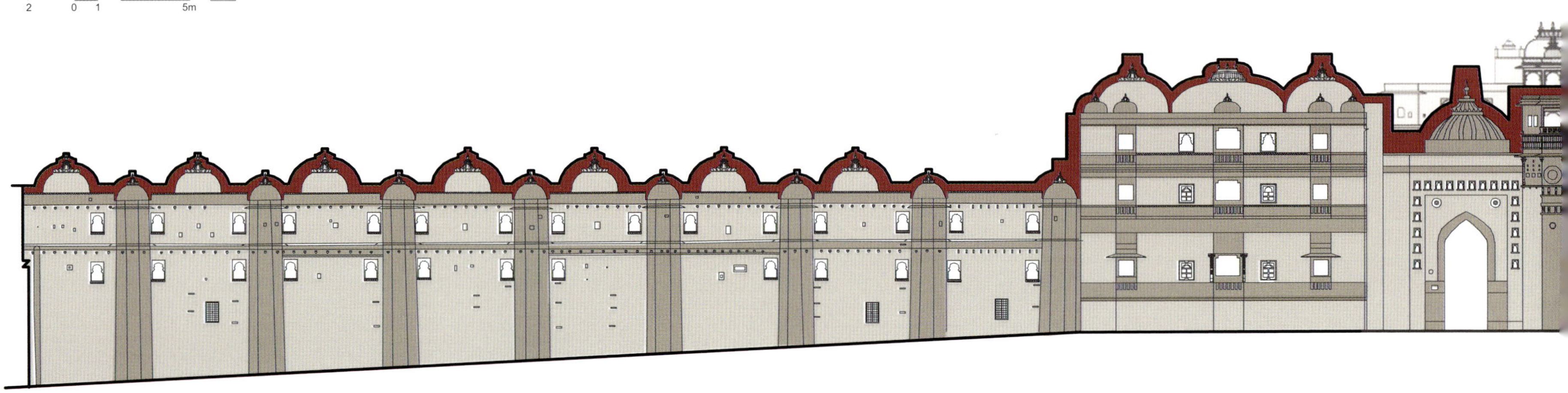

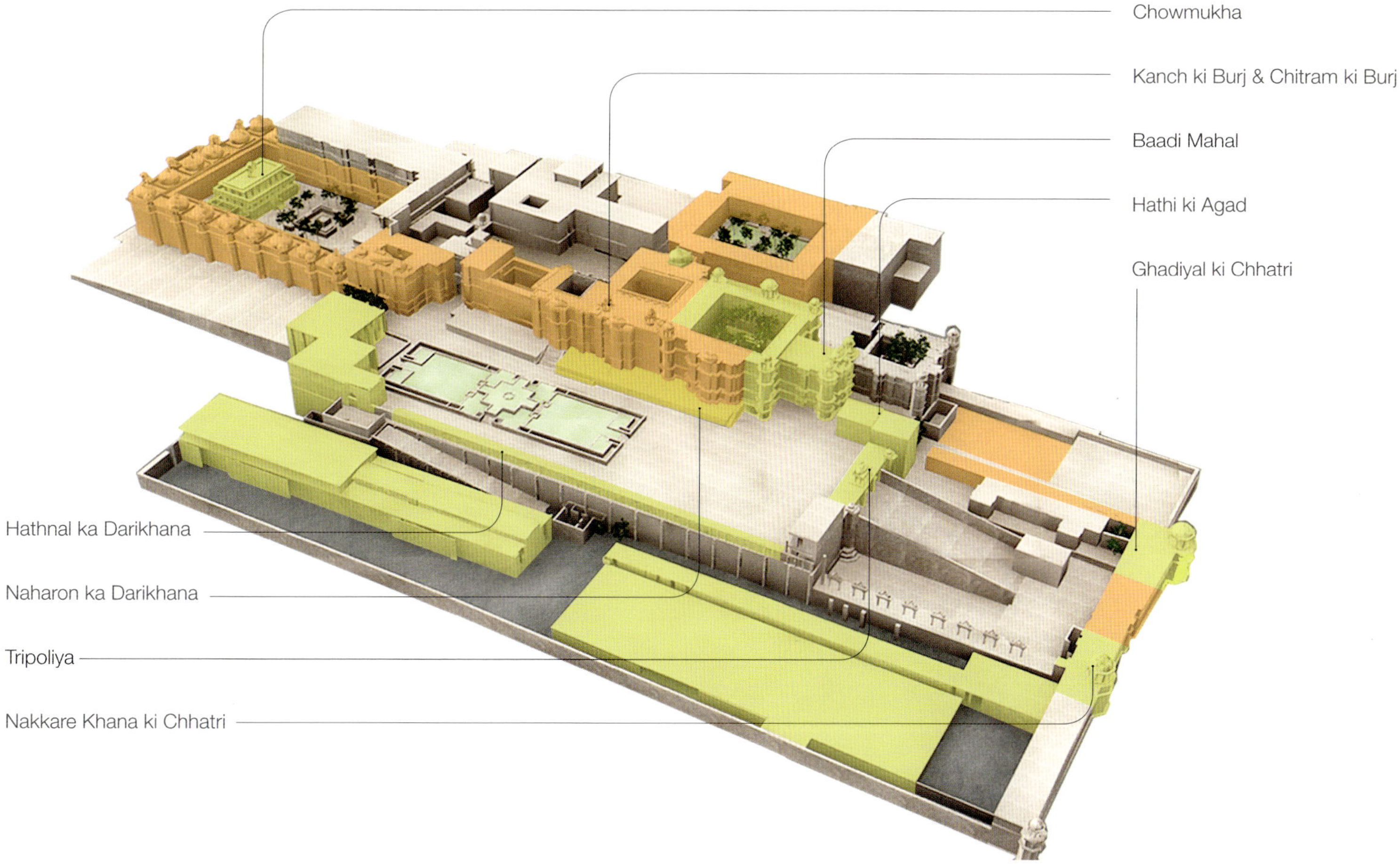

Chowmukha
Kanch ki Burj & Chitram ki Burj
Baadi Mahal
Hathi ki Agad
Ghadiyal ki Chhatri
Hathnal ka Darikhana
Naharon ka Darikhana
Tripoliya
Nakkare Khana ki Chhatri

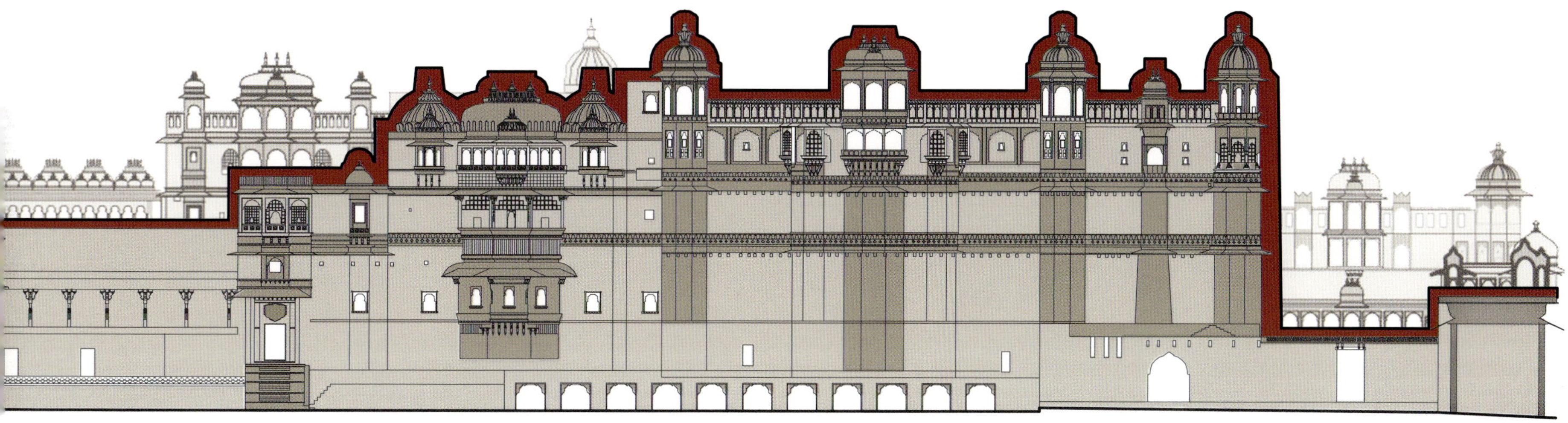

The social activities depicted in Chitram Ki Burj paintings of this phase are the only remaining evidence of the functions that were held in Rai Angan and Zenana Mahal, hence these are of exceptional cultural value. The miniature paintings are one of the rare existing visual documentation of the social festivities and urban form of the city in the 18th century. A distinct stylistic change is evident in the construction of the domed minarets, the Ghadiyal ki Chatri and the Nakkar khana ki Chatri on either side of the Badi Pol. A continuity of this architectural style is observed in the next phase of ambitious architectural additions by Maharana Sangram Singh II. This was the second attempt (after Maharana Karan Singh) to reorganise the complete City Palace. He changed the entire skyline of the City Palace by introducing large foliated domes on top of the Rai Angan block. Maharana Sangram Singh II also made several other architectural contributions in the Mewar- Mughal amalgamated styles. These include the creation of the Badi Chitrashali courtyard with smaller rooms such as the Vani Vilas on either side and the Kishan Vilas Sat Tanka on the north. Among the most important architectural contributions of this time is the creation of the magnificent Tripoliya (the triple arched gate) in line with the Badi Pol to mark the entrance to the main public space of the Manek Chowk and added the Chowmukha block - a colonnaded hall in the Lakshmi Chowk (akin to a Mughal Baradari). His architectural contributions follow the patterns of the construction of the Baadi Mahal and reflect the peak of Mewar-Mughal integration in building arts and crafts such as stone carving, *jaali* work etc.

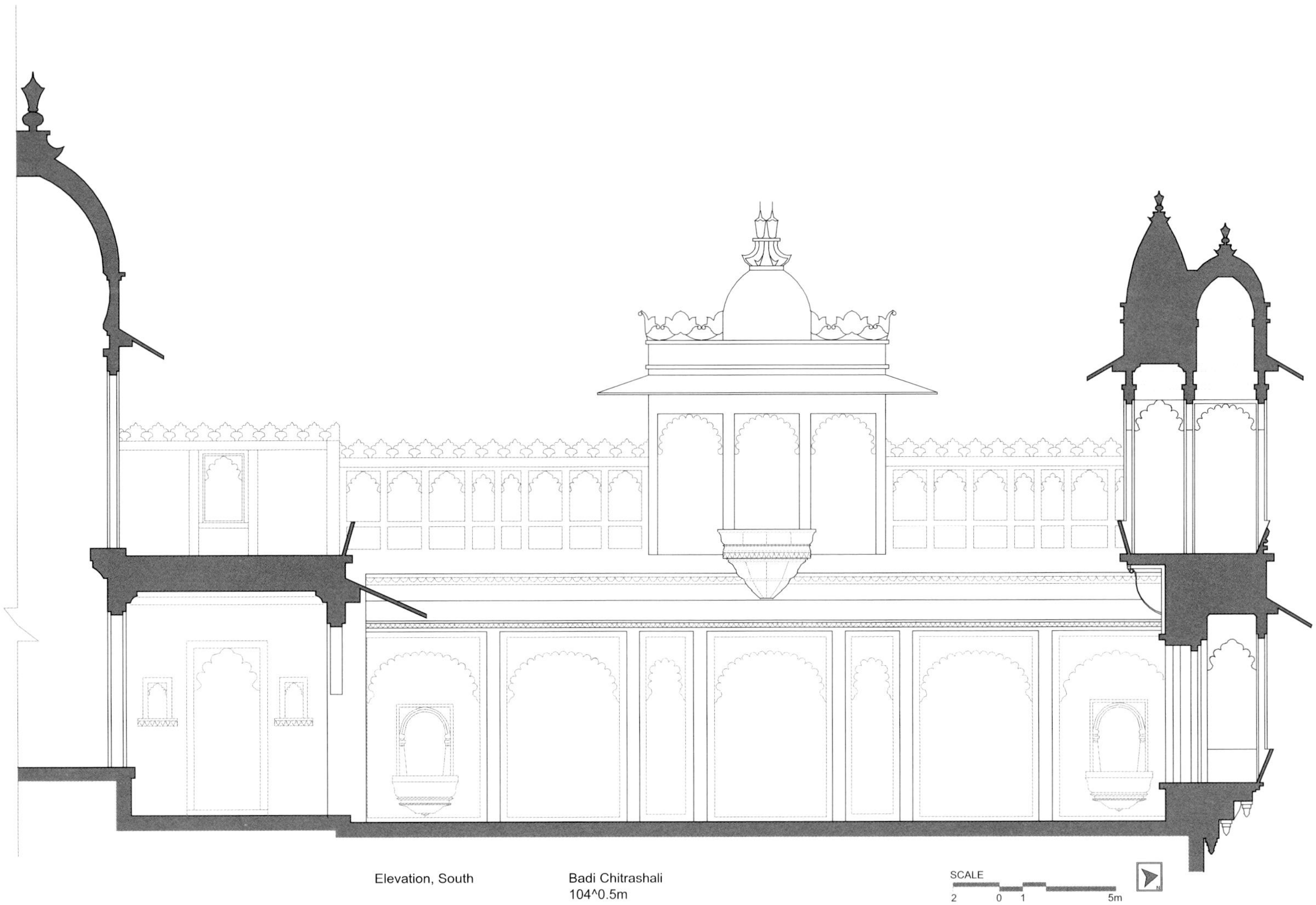

Section through Badi Chitrashali

Maharana Ari Singh II at Puja in the Shiv Prassana Amar Vilas (Baadi Mahal), Udaipur. c. 1765 by Shambhu.

Source: Freer Gallery of Art and Arthur M. Sackler Gallery, Smithsonian Institution: F1986.7, Purchase, Charles Lang Freer Endowment.

Mardana and extensions

Significant changes were made to this section of the palace in this phase, beginning from stylistic alterations that were made to one of the main gates of the Mardana, the Mardana *Deodhi*. The wide Islamic pointed arch was replaced by a much smaller cusped arch opening, the style which had become prevalent on the other gateways such as the Tripoliya and Suraj Pol. The entire skyline of this section changed significantly in this phase, due to the addition of large foliated domes, and new courtyards branching out from Rai Angan, which continued as the *genius loci* of the palace.

Moti Chowk retained most of its original character in this phase. Its usage as a connecting courtyard between the two halves of the palace also continued. The Kanwarpada ki Overi (a small room) was added to the rear of the Chowk as a storage space. Similarly, no additions or changes have been recorded in Ganesh Chowk or Satnavri Paiga in this period.

The most significant changes to the Rai Angan in this phase, were to its skyline, which had a significant impact to the external appearance of the City Palace. In the early 18th century a huge ribbed dome was added above the north room or Kacheri Mahal, which came to be used as a space for accounts work. The dome is the largest and the highest of the domes in the entire palace and is clearly discernable in the palace skyline even today. Fluted domes with finials were also added above Kaanch ki Burj and Chitram ki Burj, but the mirror work and paintings which gave these spaces their present character would be added only in the next phase.

LEFT: Exterior of the octagonal turret in Baadi Mahal

FACING PAGE: The fluted Kacheri Mahal dome above the Rai Angan

Baadi Mahal
Shiv Prasanna Amar Vilas

One of the most significant spaces architecturally, the Baadi Mahal was constructed by Maharana Amar Singh II and is formally known as the Shiv Prasanna Amar Vilas. The site possibly existed as a natural garden on a ridge in the 16th century before the Baadi Mahal palace was constructed in 1699 AD. The palace was structured to comprise of three wings around a central courtyard, though evidence of construction of a fourth wing on the south side can be observed as ground markings. It featured a beautiful central garden with flowering shrubs, trees, a water basin, fountains and arched pavilions. It was the first such courtyard of its kind in the City Palace, with a covered, colonnaded verandah and a Mughal Style Char-Bagh garden planned in conjunction.

Although the palace appears to be on the upper-most floor of the surrounding complex, it is actually built upon a hillock - a 60 ft high natural rock formation. Thus, Baadi Mahal is effectively at ground level, a fact that finds reflection in the occurrence of about 10-12 matured trees in its courtyard. The hillock is encased on all sides by high retaining walls with the one storied palace structure right on top. From the latticed windows and small *jaalis* there are magnificent views of the city to the east, and Lake Pichola with the Lake Palace on the western side. An impressive 104 carved marble columns enclose the space.

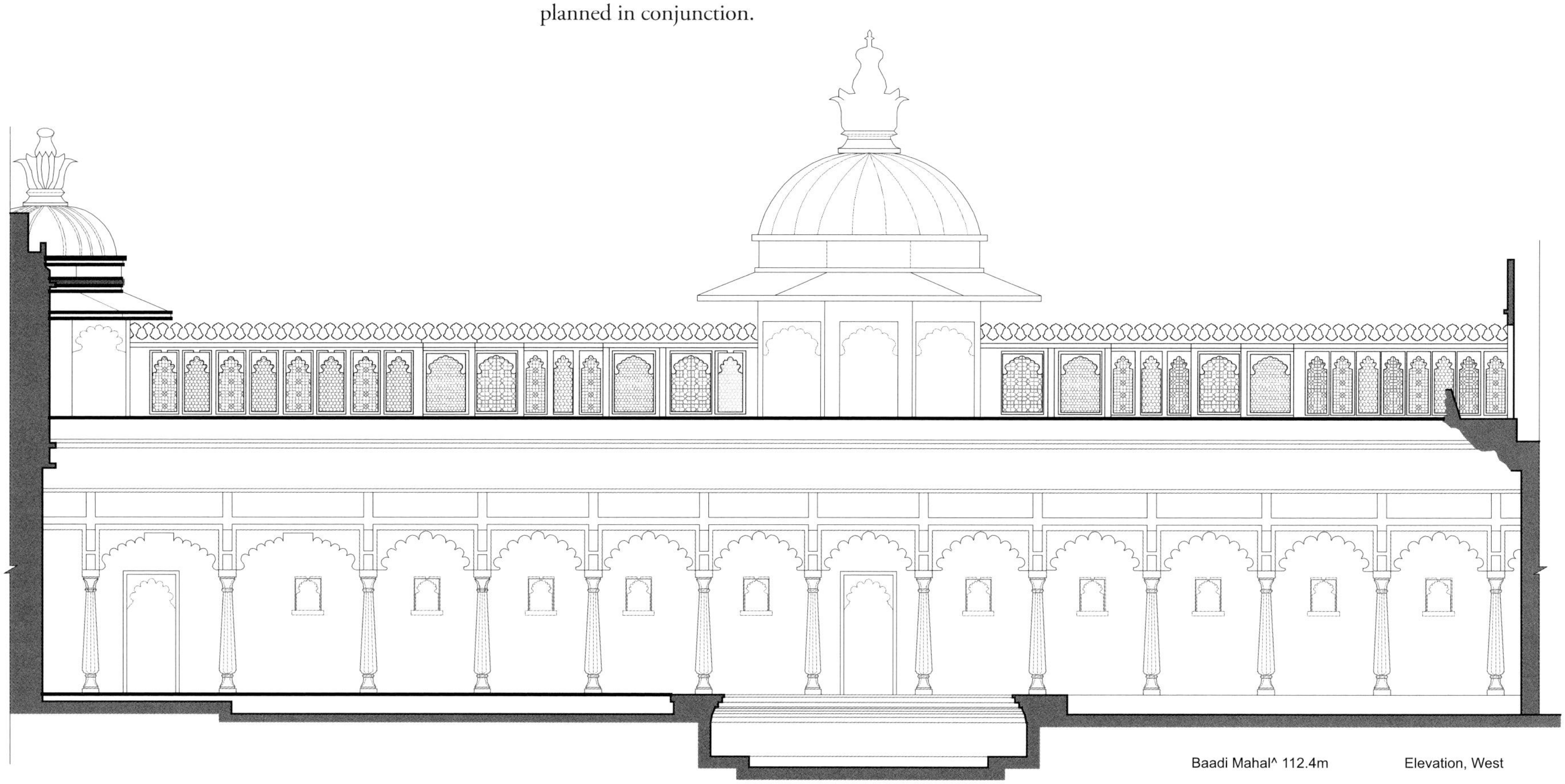

Section through Baadi Mahal

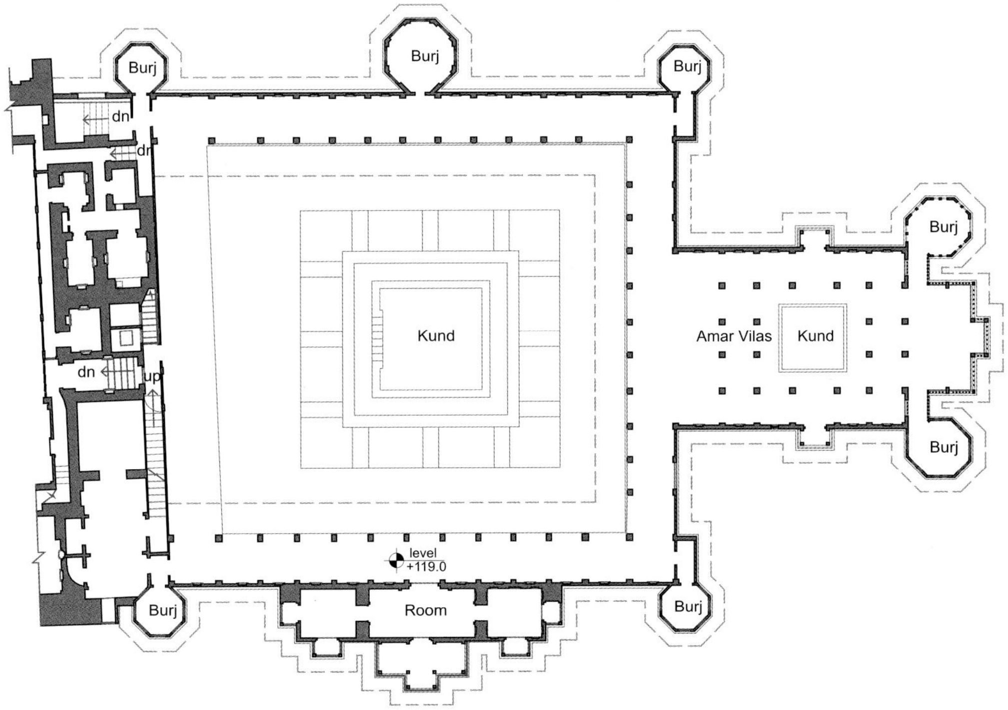

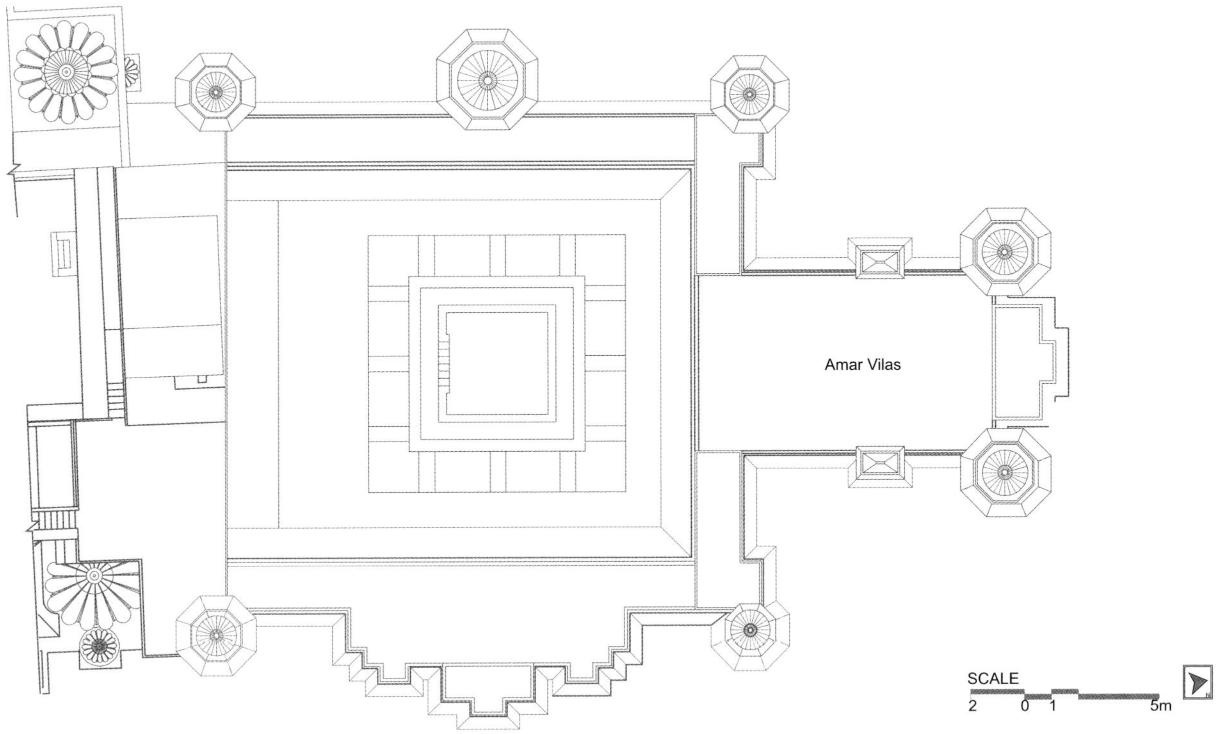

Plans of Baadi Mahal

Each column of the colonnade surrounding the court is slightly different in architectural ornamentation in terms of the carving pattern on shaft, base and capital. The elaborate carvings of these columns display excellent artistry and craftsmanship. The cusped brackets as well as the domes of the *chatris* in Baadi Mahal are uniquely representative of the Mewar-Mughal blend of architecture reaching its peak.

Water in the pool in Baadi Mahal was ensured through the technological advancements of the phase, essentially drawing the water up by a Persian wheel or simple pulley system locally known as a *rahat* or *arhat*. This mechanical system ensured the presence of water throughout the year. Moreover, the excess water was allowed to escape through an innovative design solution in the form of fountains at a much lower level near Manek Chowk, by simply using the principle of gravity. The central *chatri* on the first floor of the northern wing of the Baadi Mahal known as the Mukut Mandir was built as part of the entire palace keeping in symmetry with other octagonal and central *chatris* of all wings of the Baadi Mahal. The *chatri* was enclosed as an infill wall with small square openings as in the Baadi Mahal jharokha below at a later date.

Like Manek Chowk and Mor Chowk, Baadi Mahal is well represented through many contemporary paintings. It appears to be a favourite private palace of the Maharanas and associated with various socio-religious activities like Vaishnava recitation, celebration of *Holi* and various other festivals by the Maharanas in different periods. The central garden and vegetation changed in the 18th and 19th century, but the essential character of the Baadi Mahal as a pleasure palace as the pinnacle of the City Palace, both literally and figuratively remains unchanged even today.

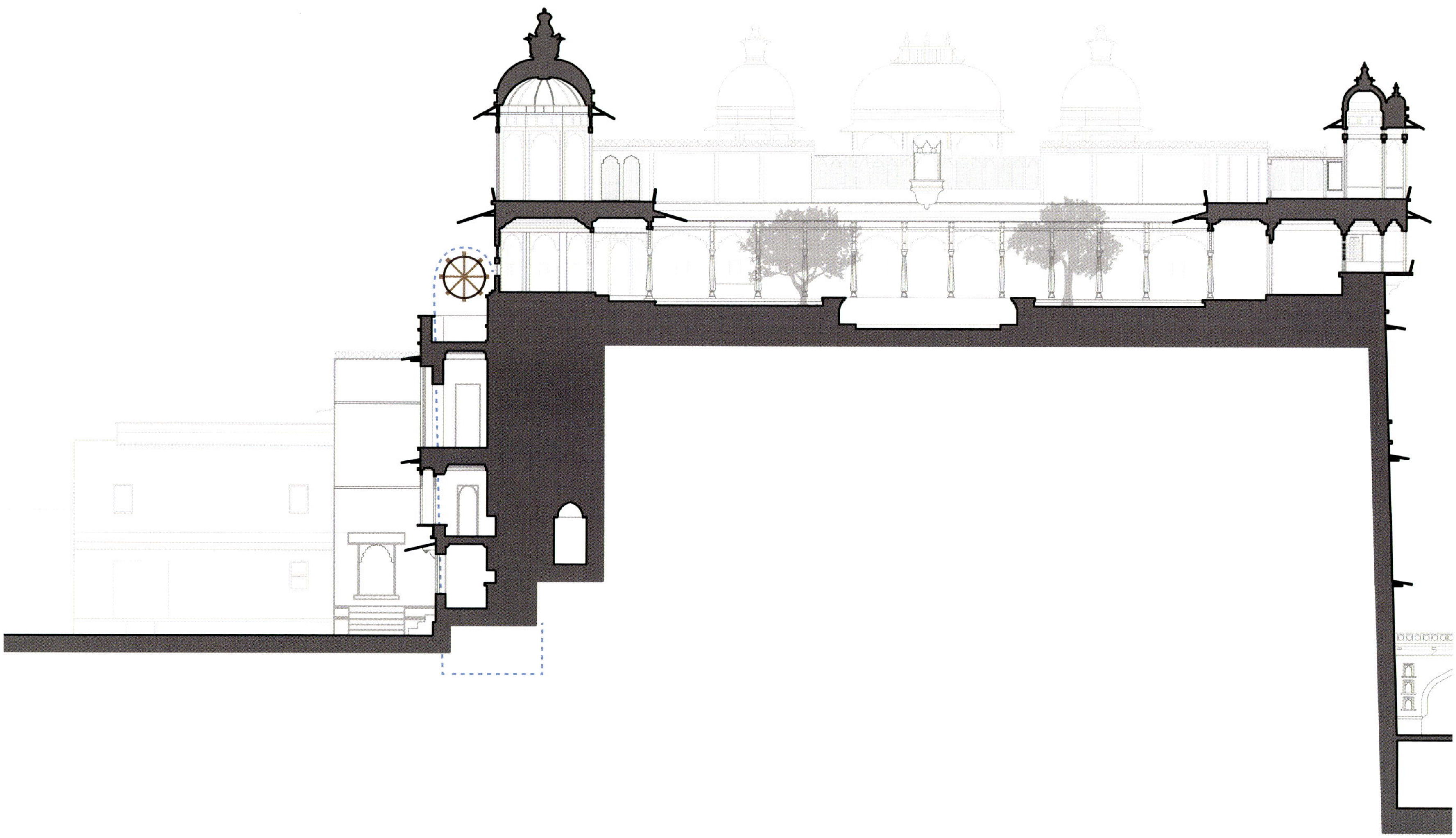

A section through Baadi Mahal showing the Persian water systems known locally as rahat or arhat.

Elevation of Mukut Mandir

Badi Chitrashali

Maharana Sangram Singh II added a new courtyard to the Mardana section, east of Moti Chowk, with the adjacent chambers Badi Chitrashali on the eastern side and Kishan Vilas Sat Tanka to the north. This court was reserved for smaller scale celebrations and functions than those which would eventually be held at the adjoining Mor Chowk.

Kishan Vilas was heavily renovated by Maharana Bhim Singh at a later date. Shiv Vilas would also be heavily modified in the 19th century. The verandah space had a projected *jharokha* (Chini Jharokha) providing an excellent view of the city. Kishan Vilas is a colonnaded block, with seven cusped arches opening into the courtyard. The triple arched projected *jharokha*, Chini Jharokha with cusped arched openings forms an important architectural feature on the eastern facade of the City Palace located right above the main entrance of the Mardana Deodhi. The *chatris* on top are reflective of the architectural styles propagated by Maharana Sangram Singh and are distinct features in the palace skyline.

Badi Chitrashali

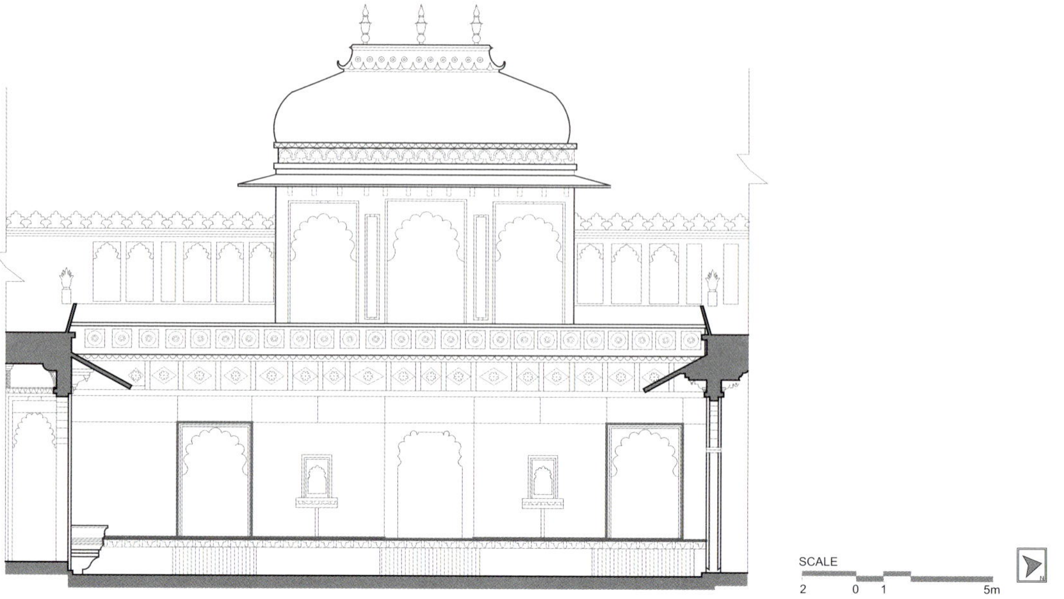

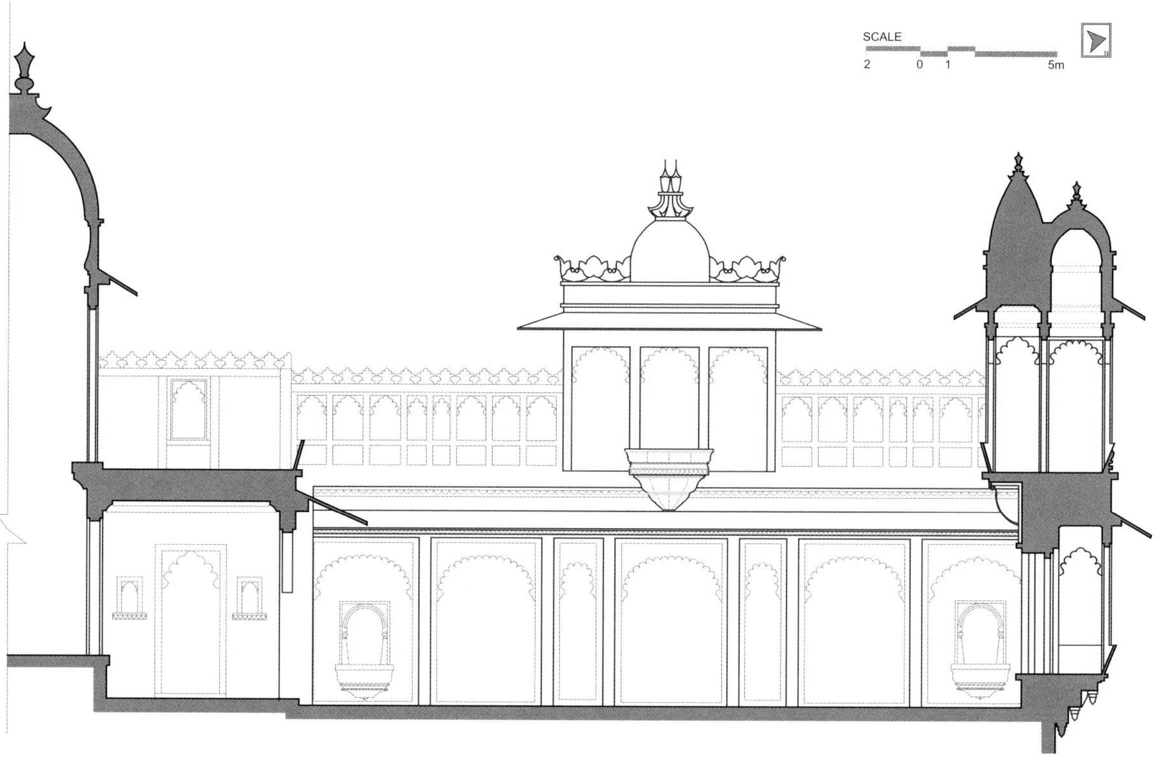

Top: West elevation of Badi Chitrashali

Above: South elevation of Badi Chitrashali

Modifications to Mor Chowk

Due to its significance as a Durbar space and as a courtyard reserved for the most elaborate of functions and festivities, this courtyard also finds depiction in a large number of Rajput paintings of different periods. A close study of these reveals the usage pattern as well as the architectural evolution in the surrounding structures of this *chowk*. Cultural performances, special *durbars* with nobles, where special guests were received marking historic turning points were all held in this chowk. Hence, even though no significant contribution to the Mor Chowk can be attributed to this phase, the *chowk* itself continued to be used as a *durbar* space and a space for celebration of special royal occasions.

Maharana Jagat Singh II attending Raaslila performance in Mor Chowk, Udaipur. c. 1736
Source: National Gallery of Victoria, Melbourne.

Zenana: Additions to Lakshmi Chowk

The Zenana Mahal which had taken shape in the previous phase shows relatively few additions in this period and a continuation of the Mewar style as opposed to the dramatic changes in the Mardana. The exact reasons for this are unclear, but elements like columns and beams continued to be constructed in the older style. For instance, in the Bhandar chowk, no significant changes were recorded in the Mewar Mughal Mature Phase, except for the change of use of the Amar Mahal as a treasury, records of which may be traced to Maharana Ari Singh II's reign.

Chowmukha, which is a pavilion located at the southern end of the Lakshmi Chowk was one of the most significant changes to the Zenana in this phase. Built during the reign of Maharana Sangram Singh II, it was intended as a space for the royal ladies to hold their own *durbar* and also serve as a space for festive occasions and ceremonies. The architectural styles for the carved stone columns are similar to the earliest 16th century columns found in Rai Angan and Zenana wings though the proportions reveal that they are18th century replicas possibly made to match with the columns in the Zenana palace wings.

The Zenana block around the Lakshmi Chowk was extended during the reign of Maharana Sangram Singh II, through the addition of an upper floor and expansion of the existing rooms. A colonnaded bay was added to the ground floor of the West wing as well.

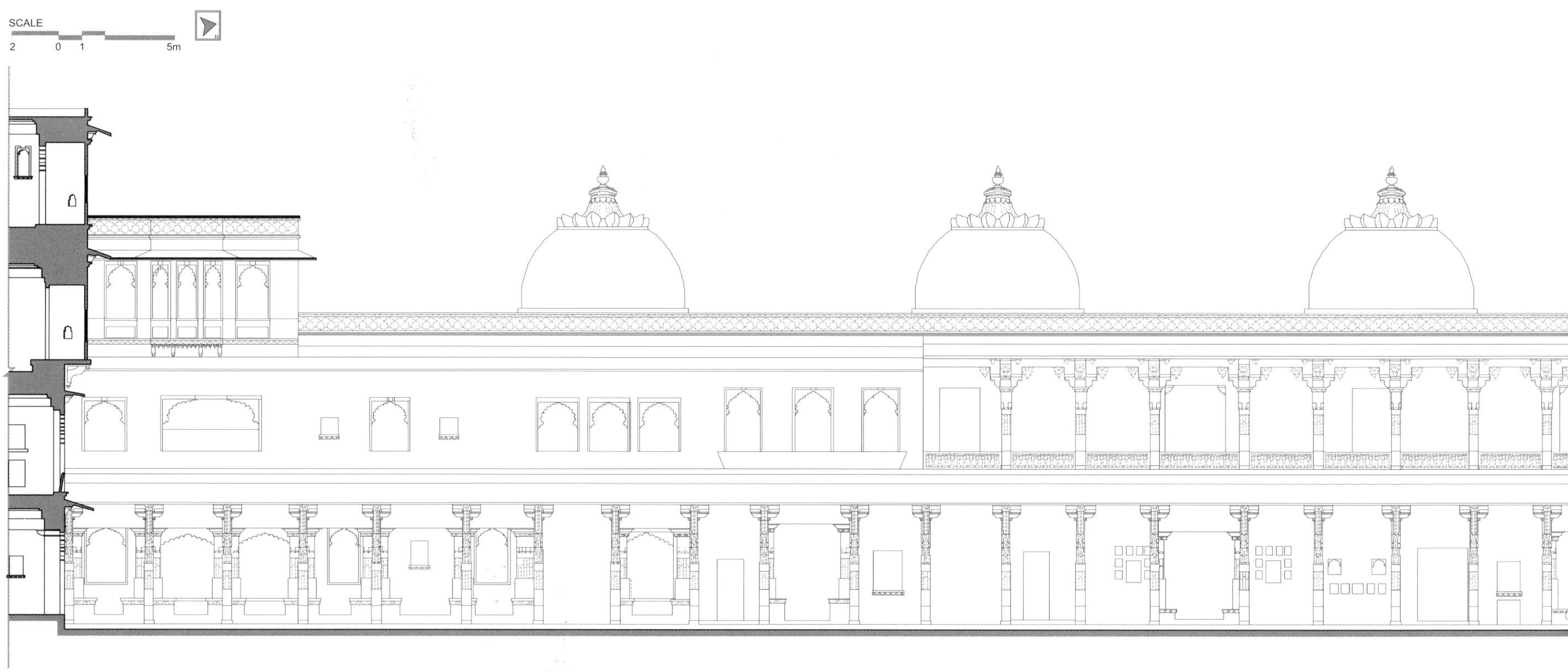

Elevation of Zenana Mahal, East side

View of Zenana Mahal

Colonnade of the Chowmukha pavilion

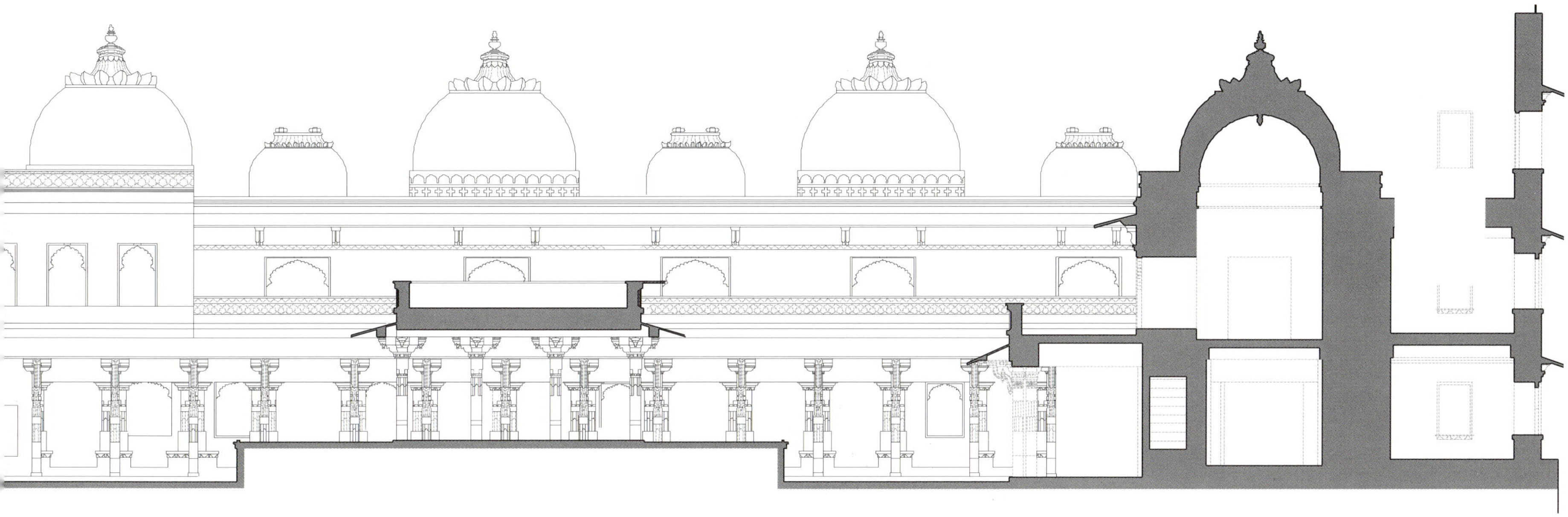

Peripheral Spaces
Badi Pol

One of the initial attempts at deviating from the pre-existing architectural expression in the City Palace can be seen in the form of the two octagonal towers which were added to Badi Pol. Both towers were capped with foliated domes with finials, and had an immediate visual impact on the first outer gate of the City Palace which had been constructed in the early 17th century in the Mewar style. The *chatri* on the east side was called the Nakkar khana ki Chatri since the turret was used to house the *nakkara* or drum which served to announce visitors to the palace as well as for welcoming guests, making announcements etc. The *chatri* on the west side, known as the Ghadiyal ki Chatri had a water clock housed within it to announce the time to the entire city. Both *chatris* were built to a height of six storeys, with the first 3 stories as solid earth, with retaining walls, and usable space on the upper two storeys with cusped arch opening on all eight sides. The foliated dome with the *kalash* (finial) is almost one storey high and marks the distinct skyline of the palace. Stylistically, the cusped arches and the domes were constructed identical to the ones in the Baadi Mahal, and reflect the strong Mughal influence on Mewar architecture, at the beginning of the 18th century. Two dalans or platforms were also added to the Badi Pol entrance.

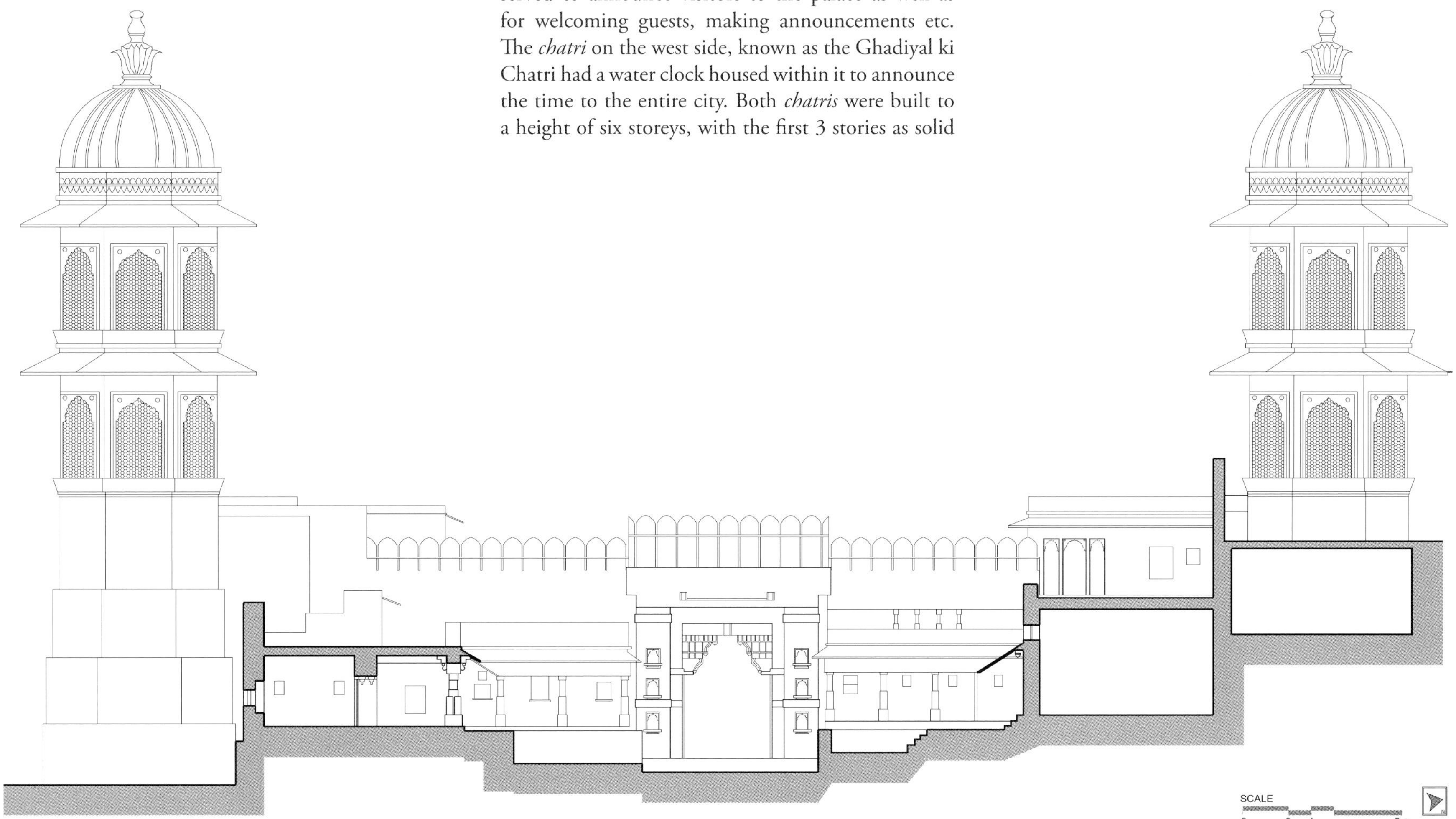

Elevation of Badi Pol

Tripoliya

The Tripoliya gate, so named because of its triple arched opening, was built in 1711 during the reign of Maharana Sangram Singh II. It was located axially behind the Badi Pol and is in perfect symmetry with it. Paintings exist before the 18th century indicating the presence of some kind of gateway prior to the Tripoliya, however there is no conclusive evidence to prove this. The new gateway became the defining edge of the Manek Chowk, giving it a grandeur and sense of arrival which continues to impress visitors to the palace today. The three cusped arch openings with niches on either side are representative of the Mughal Mewar architectural style propagated in the early 18th century. The cusped arches in the lower openings are used more as brackets with a deliberate gap in the centre. At this stage there was no upper storey to the Tripoliya which was added at a later date. A Hanuman Temple was also constructed adjacent to the Tripoliya, before entering into the Manek Chowk.

Compared to the Badi Pol gateway which has a single entrance, and which is therefore proportionally much stouter the Tripoliya has a refined sense of proportion due to its division into three distinct gateways. The difference in architectural vocabulary can be clearly seen in the two gates.

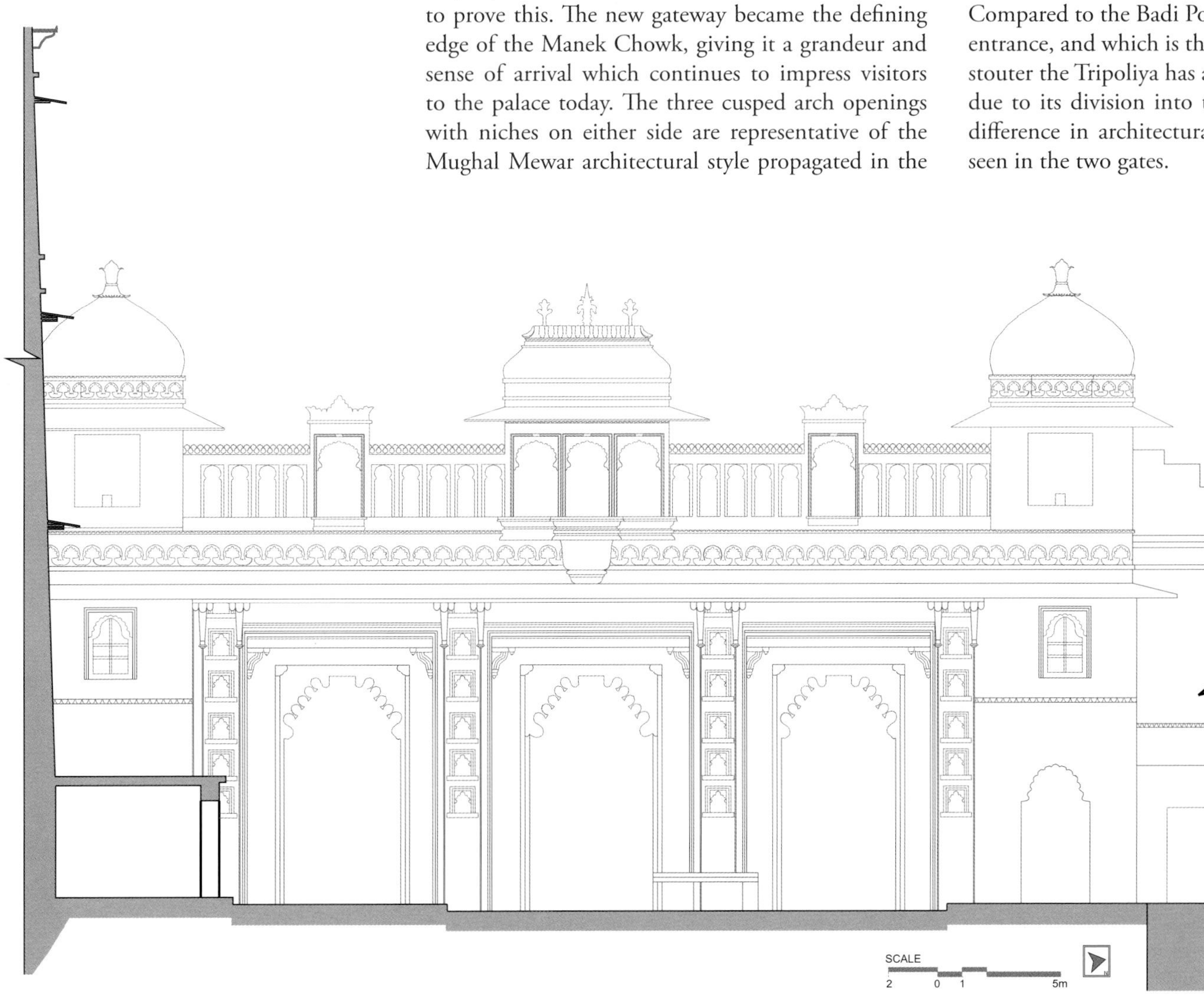

Section through Manek Chowk showing Tripoliya

Manek Chowk

Manek Chowk, which became much more defined as a public entrance courtyard with the addition of the Tripoliya continued to be at the heart of the public occasions and festivals celebrated at the City Palace. Minor additions were made to the *chowk* itself; Maharana Sangram Singh II commissioned the addition of a Hathi ka *Agad* and Hathi *Baithak* for the sport of wrestling elephants in the Manek Chowk Darikhanas.

The addition of Palkikhana is also a contribution attributed to the reign of Maharana Sangram Singh II. As the name indicates, this space was most likely created for the storage and upkeep of the *palkis* which were the traditional covered carriages used to carry royal ladies and brides. The space is marked as *daftar* (office) and Bhimsingh Chondawat ki Ori (storage space of a noble) in the 18th century map of the palace. It basically served as a service space near the Suraj Pol. The Suraj Pol itself shows great stylistic similarity with the Tripoliya, and even though its existence predates the Mewar Mughal phase, thus there can be no doubt that several significant changes and additions were made to it during the reign of Maharana Sangram Singh.

On the other side of Manek Chowk, the Toran Pol retained most its form and style, however the dome above the gateway was concealed by the additions of high parapet walls, and room with a projected *jharokha*, possible dating to 1734-54 AD.

Thus, toward the end of the 18th century, the City Palace had evolved to contain three distinct zones:

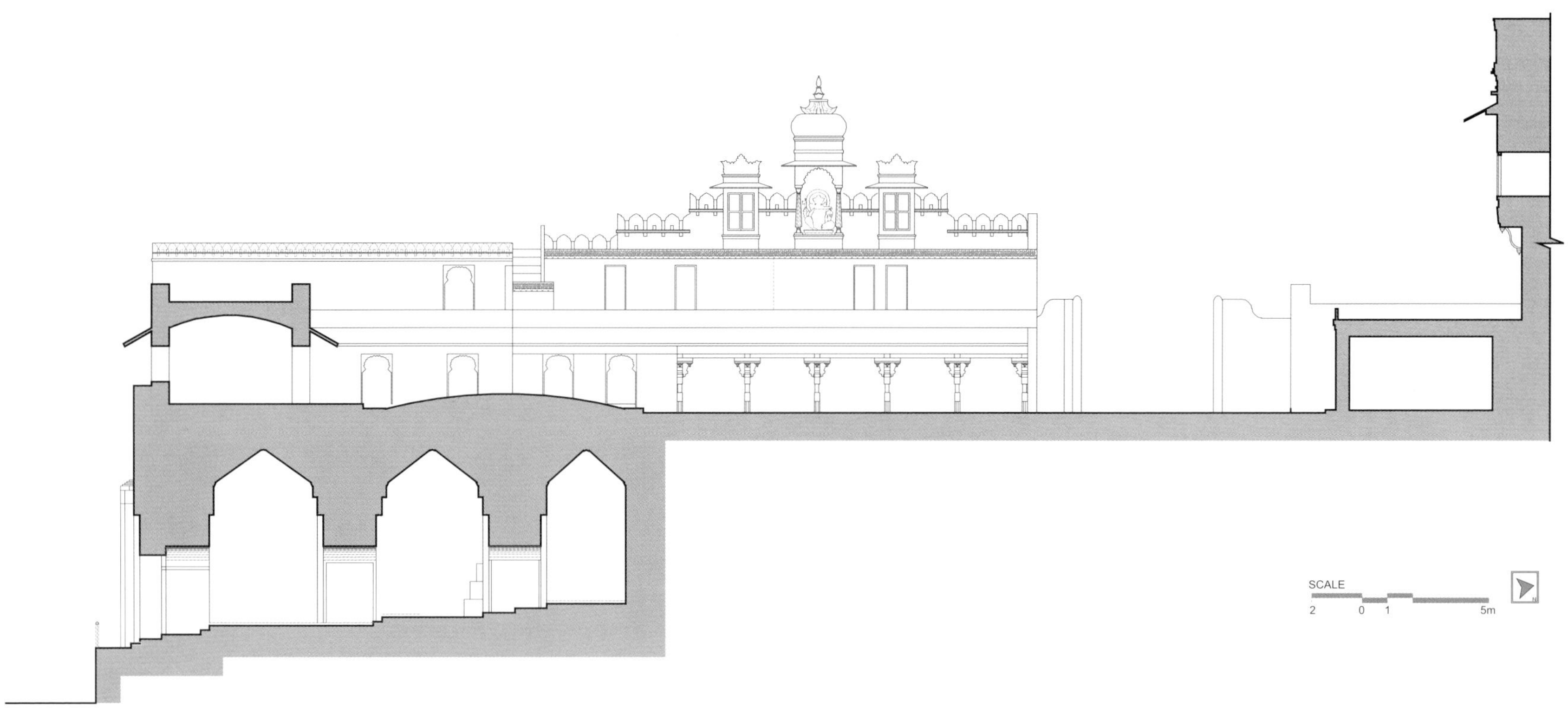

Section through Manek Chowk with Palkikhana in the background

the Mardana—which contained most of the royally significant spaces, official rooms as well as pleasure palaces and courts; the Zenana—which now housed all the royal ladies and their coterie and functioned as a parallel women's court; and the outer courtyards to the eastern periphery of the palace, comprising chiefly of the Manek Chowk which formed the public realm between the Maharana and the citizens of Udaipur. This configuration still exists today, and the visitor experience of the spaces begins with the peripheral areas, moving towards the Moti Chowk and then entering the inner palaces and courts within the palace. In the next phase, new structures and spaces were added towards the southern end, as the final phase of expansion in the City Palace.

Left: Maharana Bhupal Singh of Udaipur watching Elephant Fight at Hathi Agad, The City Palace, Udaipur, 1930-1948 CE, Acc. No: 2009.10.0243-00148

Below: View of Manek Chowk with Elephants, The City Palace, Udaipur, 1900-1915 CE, Acc. No: 2008.07.0067

Maharana Bhupal Singh of Udaipur's accession darbar at Sabha Shiromani Ka Darikhana, The City Palace, Udaipur, August 1930 CE, Acc. No: 2008.06.0429

Colonial Interactions and Final Phase of Expansion

Mewar–British Phase

The fourth phase in the development of the City Palace extends from the reign of Maharana Bhim Singh (r. 1778-1828 AD) to that of Maharana Fateh Singh (r. 1884 – 1930 AD). The political alliance of Mewar with the East India Company was accompanied by the adaption of certain British ideas of planning and architecture within the existing styles, examples of which are best seen in the additions made to Mor Chowk within the Mardana and the interiors of the new rooms added in the Zenana Mahal. The British influence on the palace is evident in architectural details such as the semicircular arch integrated with the earlier Mewar arch. The new palace structures in the vicinity of the palace complex such as the Khush Mahal, Shiv Niwas, Shambu Niwas and Fateh Prakash Palace are of Mewar British vocabulary. The interior settings also show significant features of this period such as chandeliers, chairs, toilet seats and an elevator of this time. The courtyards incorporated fountains that worked with piped water supply and had landscape features reminiscent of the English gardens.

British Influences and City Development

Minor additions were made during the reign of Maharana Bhim Singh and a few small additions were also made by the next Maharana Jawan Singh, however, the major architectural achievements in this phase may be attributed to the reign of Maharana Swarup Singh and later, to Maharana Sajjan Singh. Swarup Singh's architectural achievements include adding new structures to pre-existing ones, such as the Hawa Mahal over Tripoliya, the Yash Mandir above Baadi Mahal, Surya Prakash and Swarup Vilas on Mor Chowk eastern facade, and the creation of a new palace—Khush Mahal, among other additions. The later period developments of this century saw several additions beyond the extents of the City Palace, such as the Shambhu Niwas. A further expansion could be seen in the form of the Shiv Niwas Palace, which now forms the southernmost part of the complex, by Maharana Sajjan Singh. The new palaces of Shambhu Niwas and Shiv Niwas reflect the integration of the planning principles from the British period replacing traditional courtyards with monumental forms with wide spans and experimental shapes, high ceilings as in British bungalows were created. At the same time, European inspired methods of decoration, such as glass work and enamel work were introduced within the pre-existing spaces of the palace. The magnificent ornamentation in Mor Chowk may be attributed to Maharana Sajjan Singh reign and it remains one of the finest expressions of the additive character of the City Palace, showing influences of Mughal and British styles on the typical Mewar style of planning.

Towards the end of the 18th century, Udaipur was in a precarious position financially as well as politically. The Maratha incursions and internal dissent were mostly responsible for the sorry state of affairs. Maharana Ari Singh's younger son Bhim Singh (r. 1778-1828 AD) succeeded Hamir Singh in 1778 AD among continuing internal dissension and civil strife. Driven to dire financial straits and facing internal troubles, the Maharana and his councillor began to look towards the option of entering into a Subsidiary Alliance Treaty with the East India Company.

Following negotiations, a treaty was signed on 13th January 1818. According to these negotiations, the Mewar ruler agreed to act in cooperation with the East India Company. At this point, Captain (later Lt. Colonel) James Tod, recently appointed the first Political Agent of Mewar drafted an agreement or *Kaul-nama* to bring about an understanding between the nobles and the Maharana. The agreement helped establish the notion of the absolute supremacy of the Maharana over his chiefs and kinsmen, in place of the long established custom of regarding the ruler as 'first among equals'.

For a short time at least, interim peace was finally established in a wallowing state. With the temporary revival in economic conditions and political stability, the Maharana could focus on construction work within the City Palace as well as in

Maharana Bhim Singh
AD 1778 - 1828

Maharana Jawan Singh
AD 1828 - 1838

Maharana Sardar Singh
AD 1838 - 1842

Maharana Swarup Singh
AD 1842 - 1861

Udaipur. One of the first additions to the palace in his reign and in this phase was the addition of the Hawa Mahal, built by Maharana Swarup Singh in 1842-1861 AD, a screened structure with ornate carvings above Tripoliya Gate, built in 1711 AD. Some of the earlier palace spaces built by Maharana Karan Singh and Sangram Singh II were renovated by him as well. The Sat Tanka was renamed as Krishna Vilas, a memorial shrine dedicated to Maharana Bhim Singh's sixteen year old daughter named Krishna Kumari who had sacrificed her life to end the conflict between the warring states of Mewar, Marwar and Dhoondhar. Within the city, the Maharana added structures such as the Maha Kali ka Mandir, Naya Mahal and Parvati Vilas.

Maharana Bhim Singh was succeeded by his son, Jawan Singh (r.1828-1838 AD). The financial condition of Mewar, which had already begun to decline again in the past few years, worsened in his reign and within a few years, as had happened before, the State was heavily in debt and the tribute due to the British had fallen into arrears. Maharana Jawan Singh, during his short reign lavishly ornamented the interiors of Moti Mahal, originally the private residential palace of Maharana Karan Singh. A connection was also opened up through the addition of stairs from the Moti Mahal to Baadi Mahal. He also made some minor additions to Choti Chitrashali and the Toran Pol. Within the city, work on the Jal Niwas progressed and a structure known as the Jawan Burj was added.

The eastern façade of The City Palace, Udaipur, 1910 CE, Acc. No: 2008.07.0062

Maharana Shambhu Singh
AD 1861 - 1874

Maharana Sajjan Singh
AD 1874 - 1884

Maharana Fateh Singh
AD 1884 - 1930

Major Expansions and Administrative Reforms

Maharana Jawan Singh passed the *gaddi* of Mewar on to Sardar Singh (r. 1838-1842 AD), a decision which was approved by the East India Company. His reign was short-lived and beleaguered with political strife, so it is unsurprising that no construction in the palace is recorded in this period. Maharana Sardar Singh was succeeded by Swarup Singh (r. 1842-1861 AD). He introduced several administrative reforms in an attempt to bolster the financial condition of the state. He also invested in the construction of lakes and palaces within the city, since the conditions in Udaipur came back to some semblance of order. Among his contributions were the Akhare ka Mahal, Pitamabar Rai ka Devalaya, Gulab Swaroop Bihari ka Mandir, Arsi Vilas, Goverdhan Vilas and the Magri ka Darikhana.

Maharana Swarup Singh oversaw the third major expansion campaign of the City Palace after his predecessors Maharana Karan Singh and Maharana Sangram Singh II. He made substantial changes in the City Palace and added a number of new palatial structures in a unique Mewar- British style, often seen as part of Indo-Saracenic building activities which had become popular in most princely states by this time. These include the construction of Yash Mandir above Baadi Mahal, Surya Prakash and Swarup Vilas on the eastern facade of Mor Chowk, and creation of Khush Mahal. The Ganesh Mandir above Palkikhana was also added by him. Additionally, he created the Darikhana above Moti Chowk Paiga on the upper level of Moti Chowk, in line with Ganesh Chowk, significantly changing the spatial character of the *chowk*. Various other activities, of re-plastering exterior and interior spaces and minor additions to several spaces have also been recorded in this period. Maharana Swarup Singh died in 1861, and was succeeded by his adopted nephew, Shambhu Singh (r. 1861-1874 AD). The trend set by Maharana Swarup Singh with regards to the administrative and political reforms continued with the reign of Maharana Shambhu Singh, despite opposition from his court, and political rivalries. Among the improvements was the construction of several roads within the city , a *sarai* near Suraj Pol and Hathi Pol, the addition of Shambhu Prakash Mahal in Jagniwas and perhaps most significantly, the introduction of Shambhuratna Pathshalas or schools in Udaipur.

A view of Sajjangarh on Basandra Hills, Udaipur Acc. No: 2009.09.0159-00006

The Maharana was responsible for continuing the new phase of expansion and addition to the palace undertaken by his uncle. Shambhu Niwas, which was a complete and independent palace in itself, was added south of Lakshmi Chowk, and Shiv Niwas, a palace adjacent to it was also begun at this time. Kamal Pol was constructed to the south of the City Palace. He ordered several small changes to both the Mardana and Zenana spaces in the existing palace; the Badi Chitrashali was modified to include Saraswati Bhandar (now Vani Vilas) and the Amar Mahal, which had remained mostly unchanged for over a century was also expanded with the addition of Badal Mahal or a Monsoon Room, on the top most level. He also added Basant Chowk to the palace's courtyards. His contributions to the City Palace significantly expanded the built form and skyline of the palace. After the demise of Maharan Shambhu Singh in 1874, his first cousin Sajjan Singh (r. 1874-1884 AD) was invested with ruling powers. Land taxation system had also become fairly sophisticated. Other administrative reforms marked Sajjan Singh's reign. Udaipur became the second city after Bombay to form a municipality. Plans were drawn up to desilt Lake Pichola and afforestation programmes were launched.

Maharana Sajjan Singh also undertook ambitious projects in construction within the city such as Badi Pal Dam and Sajjan Niwas Garden, locally known as Gulab Bagh. The Sajjan Niwas Garden was envisioned as a large scale public park within the now dense fabric of Udaipur. He also commissioned the construction of Sajjan garh on the peak of Bansdara Hill as a summer retreat for the Maharanas, and its common nickname as the Monsoon Palace points to its location on a vantage point where the advancing monsoon could be viewed at length. This venture was successful in providing employment within the city. Unfortunately it wasn't completed in his lifetime and never really acquired the stature of an inhabited palace over the years.

Within the City Palace, one of the most significant accomplishments of Maharana Sajjan Singh was the addition of the glass-work and inlay work in the Mor Chowk which makes it one of the most artistically significant spaces within the palace. He also continued work on Shiv Niwas Palace, which is the southernmost part of the complex. Maharana Sajjan Singh also established the 'Sajjan Vani Vilas' library. It was during Sajjan Singh's reign that Kaviraj Shyamaldas (1836-1893 AD), who was appointed to look after this library, wrote the major part of his now-renowned history of Mewar. The title of 'Kaviraj', or 'King of Poets', was bestowed on Shyamaldas for his skills. He is best-known for his five volume history of Mewar - the *Veer Vinod*, published by Mewar State in 1886, then suppressed, and finally released for public consumption in 1945. Maharana Sajjan Singh was succeeded by his cousin, Fateh Singh (r. 1884-1930 AD) who was also an adopted heir. His reign saw further modernisation of the administration and the opening of new educational institutions, medical facilities, roads and irrigation works. Famine-years added to the economic problems of Mewar and its general populace. Historically, the economic conditions of Mewar had been strained during the 18th & 19th centuries and with a constant increase in taxation over the decades and inability of farmers to pay debts, by the 20th century, the situation lead to popular agrarian movements. The first three decades of the 20th century saw a continuation of Maharana Fateh Singh's reign. Fateh Singh consistently took on the pro-British political faction in Mewar, and resisted attempts at modernising and the appointment of pro-British administrators and ministers. He devoted himself to developing educational institutes across the state and encouraged the introduction of railway lines from Udaipur. During his reign, a Public Works Department was set up which looked after construction, maintenance and repair of buildings. He also restored old mansions in Chittor and the palace at Kumbhalgarh, renovated and

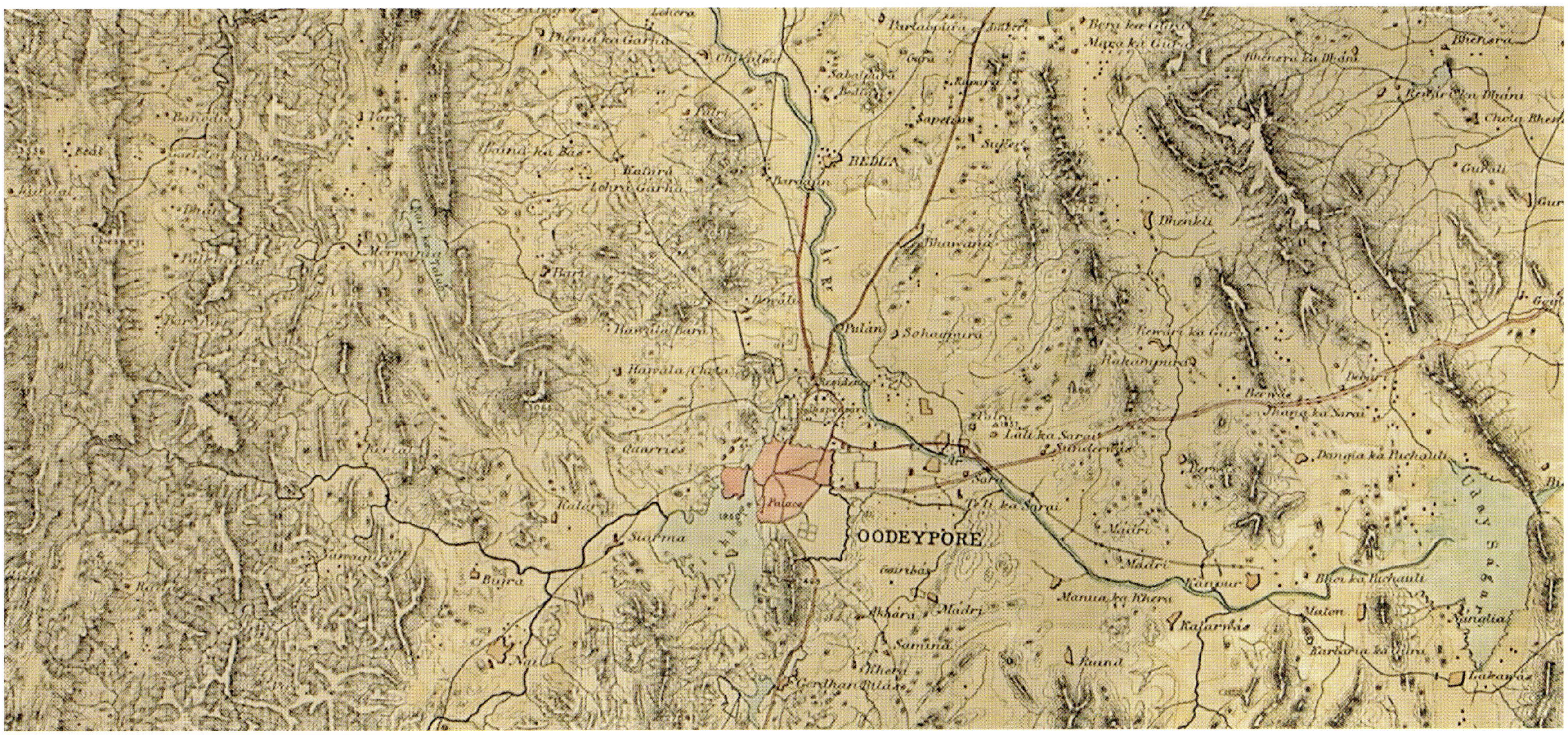

A 19th century map of Udaipur and its environs
Reference: Part of Oodeypore (Rajputana Agency) Season - 1877–78
Central India and Rajputana Survey Sheet no. 145
MMRI Map no.: MC 105 © MMCF, The City Palace, Udaipur

made additions in the City Palace at Udaipur, built the Durbar Hall (now called Fateh Prakash) and completed the Shiv Niwas Palace as a guesthouse for visitors, and extended water resources of the city by constructing the Fateh Sagar Lake. The Victoria Hall, built to commemorate Queen Victoria's jubilee was completed in 1890. Small palaces in Kumbhalgarh and Udai Sagar were also constructed in this period. A palace was also added by him in the Saheilyon ki Bari and a new palace on the band of Jaisamand.

Within the City Palace, the Maharana made additions to Shambhu Niwas; in 1906, Shiv Niwas Palace was finally completed. He also added additional buildings such as Fateh Prakash, Jas Prakash in 1910 which was in the eastern wing of Zenana Mahal. For his son, the Maharana created Bhupal Vilas and Bhupal Prakash in 1911 on the second floor of the Zenana. Apart from construction work and upgradation of the palace services, the Maharana also continued the renewal activity in the form of art work and plaster and paint works. For instance, the stucco work in Rai Angan can be attributed to this period. At the end of Maharana Fateh Singh's reign, the palace had expanded almost to its fullest extent, and retains most of its form since then.

Top: Fateh Prakash Palace
Above: View of Fateh Sagar Lake, Udaipur, 1945-1950 CE, Acc. No: 2009.10.0102-00015

19th century painting of City Palace
Image Courtesy: Media Office, Eternal Mewar, The City Palace, Udaipur, Rajasthan

This phase saw the introduction of the British influence on planning, architectural modulation of elevations as well as structural innovations and new technologies. The Shiv Niwas Palace and Fateh Prakash and Shambhu Niwas show considerable deviation from the rest of the City Palace since they were executed in the Mewar-British style. This meant the introduction of new shapes, larger spans, geometrically ordered facades. At the same time, within the older structures, there was a sense of holding on to the older traditional forms of architecture and art. For instance, the Chhota Darikhana added on the upper level of Moti Chowk was executed with the same elements as the existing structures within the chowk.

There was also significant ornamentation added to existing spaces within the palace, with Mor Chowk being one of the most opulent and aesthetically pleasing of artistic executions. The skyline of the palace saw some changes, with the addition of a second floor in the Zenana, Hawa Mahal above Tripoliya; however the change was not as dramatic as seen in the previous phases. The focus of the palace had shifted to the construction of entirely new blocks, and extending the palace south and it was these spaces that became the primary residence of the Maharanas hereafter.

Left: Decorative glass and mirror work in Mor Chowk

Below: The skyline during this phase

Facing Page: The final phase of expansion in the City Palace

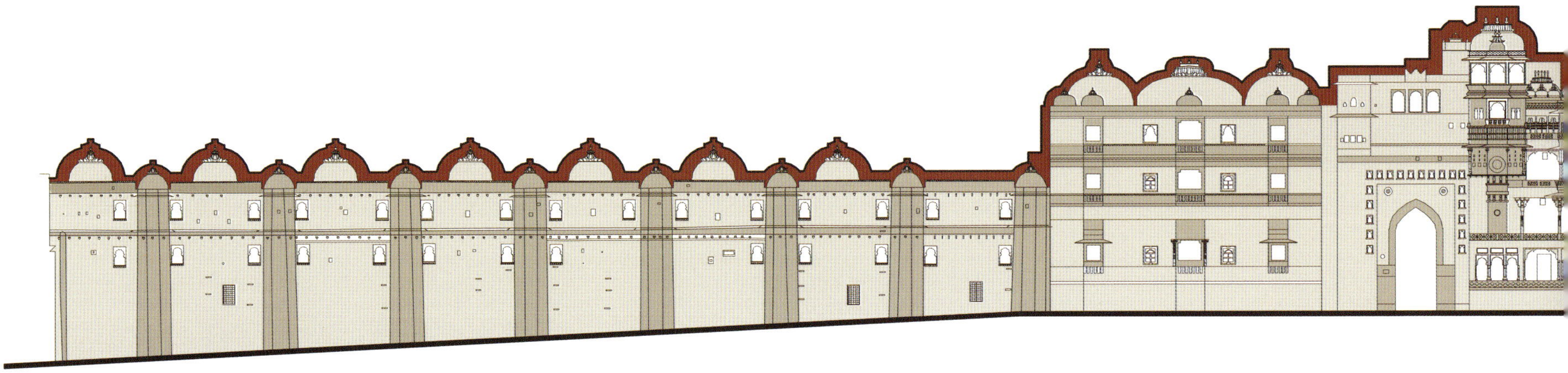

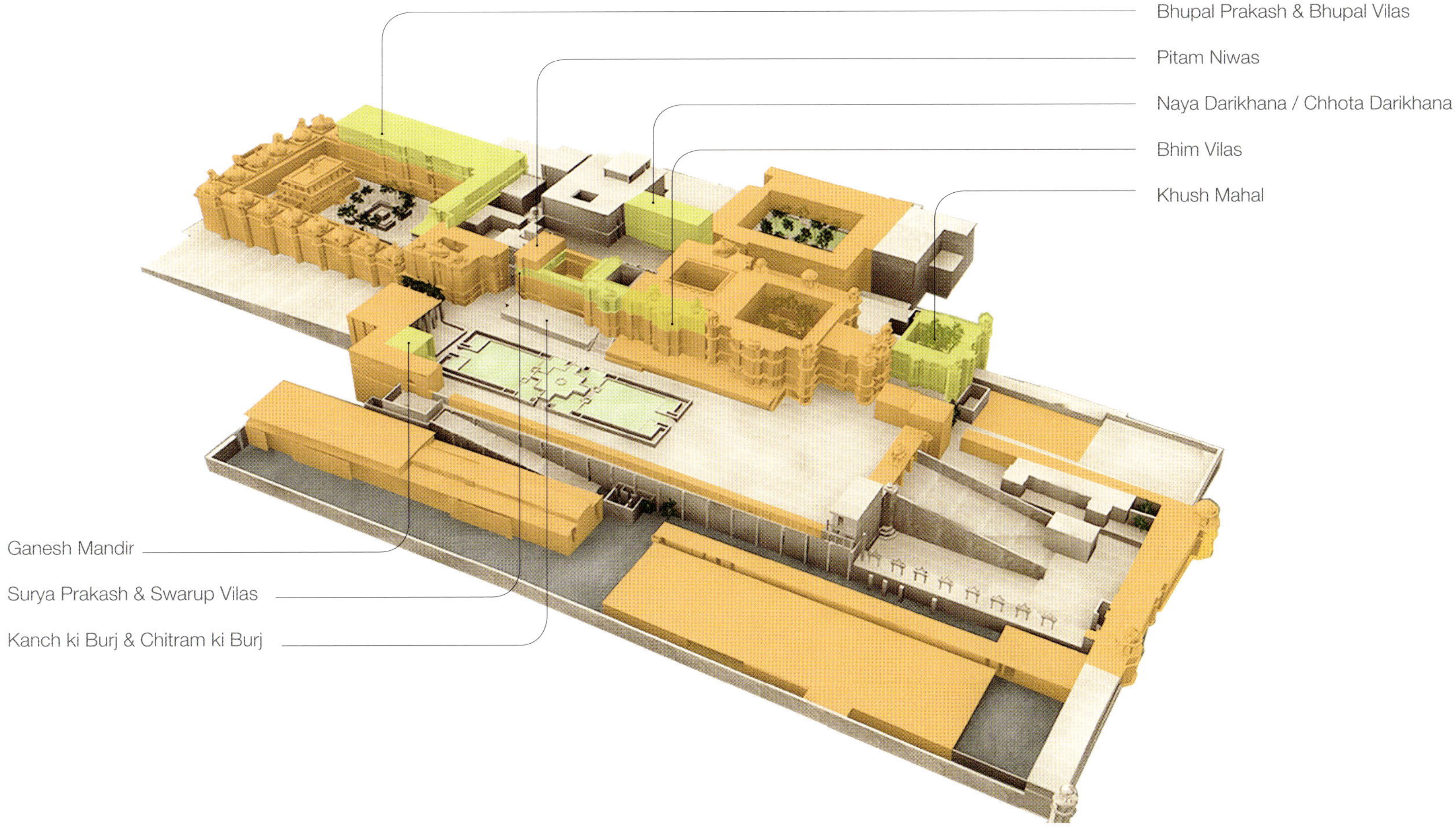
Bhupal Prakash & Bhupal Vilas
Pitam Niwas
Naya Darikhana / Chhota Darikhana
Bhim Vilas
Khush Mahal
Ganesh Mandir
Surya Prakash & Swarup Vilas
Kanch ki Burj & Chitram ki Burj

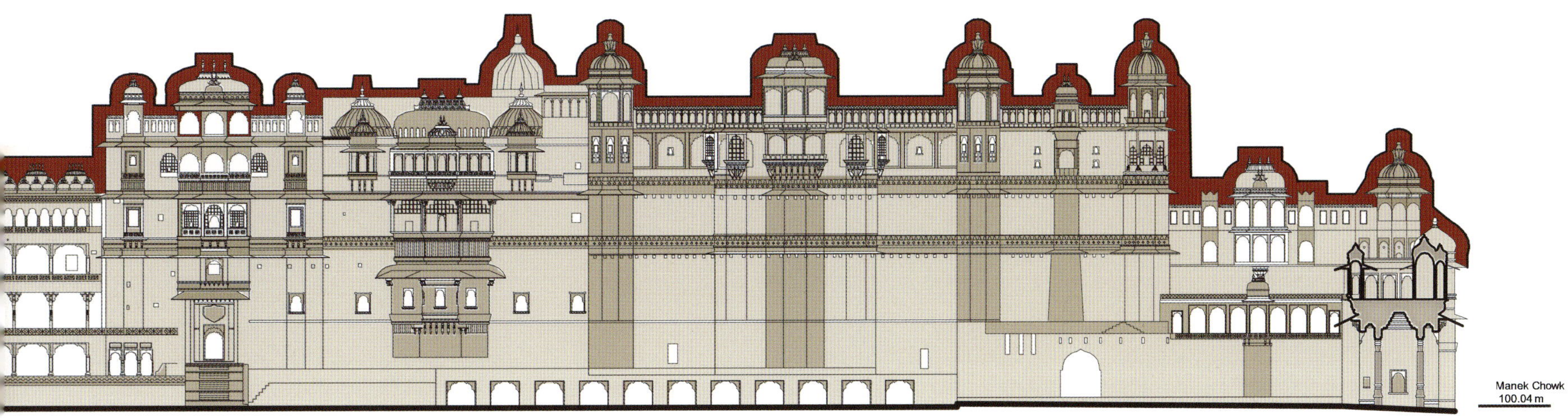
Manek Chowk
100.04 m

Mardana: Modifications and Additions

In this phase, the *bahidas*, currently housed in the Maharana Mewar Research Institute record the daily activities of the Maharanas since the 18th century and provide useful information about the cultural usage of the palatial spaces, especially in the Mardana Mahal. For instance, one finds description of festivals like *Khejri Pujan*, *Navratri* and *Rathyatra* in1780, during the reign of Maharana Bhim Singh. There are further descriptions of the festivals of *Gangaur*, *Pavitra Chodas*, *Teej*, elephant fight, *Sheetla Pujan*, and newly introduced British games. The 1810 records include descriptions of gambling games in the Darikhana. These descriptions indicate how new activities were integrated within the pre-existing spaces of the palace and the growing influence of the British, not only on the architecture and planning of the palace, but also on the lifestyles and habits of the royal family.

The layout and form of Moti Chowk and Ganesh Chowk was altered due to the addition and modification of several built spaces which surrounded it. Even though Moti Chowk continued to be a collection space for royal processions and gatherings, connecting the two main sections of the palace, new functions were added to it. For instance, the space which comprised of a small courtyard, surrounded by small rooms known previously known as Kanwarpada ki Ori (storage spaces for the Prince) was converted into Khasa Rasoda, literally translated as Special Kitchens, in the 19th century by Maharana Swarup Singh, a fact that is still evident from the existing chimneys on the roof of the first floor. Chhota Darikhana was created as a colonnaded hall for meetings above the western wing of the Satnavari Paiga and could be accessed from Ganesh Chowk as well as Moti Chowk. Chhota Darikhana or Chhota Darikhana is a nine bay double aisle space with a high parapet on the terrace. The monolithic stone columns and brackets have the basic temple style with minimal ornamentation. The cusped arch openings on the ground floor and parapets on first floor in the western block were added in the 20th century.

Mardana Deodhi, which formed a key entry point into the Mardana Mahal, constantly modified in previous phases, was modified again with the addition of the court of arms in the 20th century. Sabha Shiromani was extended through the addition of columns to create two more bays to the existing three bays lengthwise, and the addition of stone parapet and cusped arches in the niches at the lower ground level. The new columns can be differentiated from the older columns, on closer examination.

Ganesh Deodhi was heavily ornamented through the addition of glass inlay during the 19th century. The chatri of the gateway was decorated with floral work on the base and a glass finial. China tiles were added to the interiors in the 20th century.

While Rai Angan remained more or less unchanged in this phase, structurally, the Nika ki Chopad was decorated with a stucco pattern for the parapet. In Chitram ki Burj, which already had a profusion of painting and art work from the previous phase, another layer of brightly coloured paintings in Nathdwara Pichwai style can be seen, which may be attributed the reign of Maharana Bhim Singh. The exquisite glass and mirror work was added to the Kaanch ki Burj in the manner of a Sheesh Mahal during the reign of Maharana Shambhu Singh.

The central garden and vegetation changed in the 18th and then again in the 19th century. In the upper terrace of the garden, Maharana Jawan Singh enclosed the space by adding high parapets with stone *jaalis* to form an enclosed terrace space called Mukut Mandir. It was used as a leisure space by the Maharanas and provides an excellent view of the lake and the city.

Yash Mandir was created as a leisure palace by Maharana Swarup Singh on top of Baadi Mahal in the south east corner. The palace space overlooks Manek Chowk and was built to provide a panoramic view of the growing capital city below. It consists of two interconnected chambers extending in to a *jharokha* to the east. The internal walls, columns and ceilings have mirror work, with mirrors of varying sizes, reflecting the building arts of the 19th century. Besides the glass work, there is ornamentation in the form of inlay on timber and paintings on niches.

Left: Ganesh Doedhi inlay work

Below: Modifications made to the Mardana Deodhi and the additions of the court of arms

Right: Interiors of the Kaanch ki Burj

Below: Lime work and stained glass added to spaces in Chandra Mahal

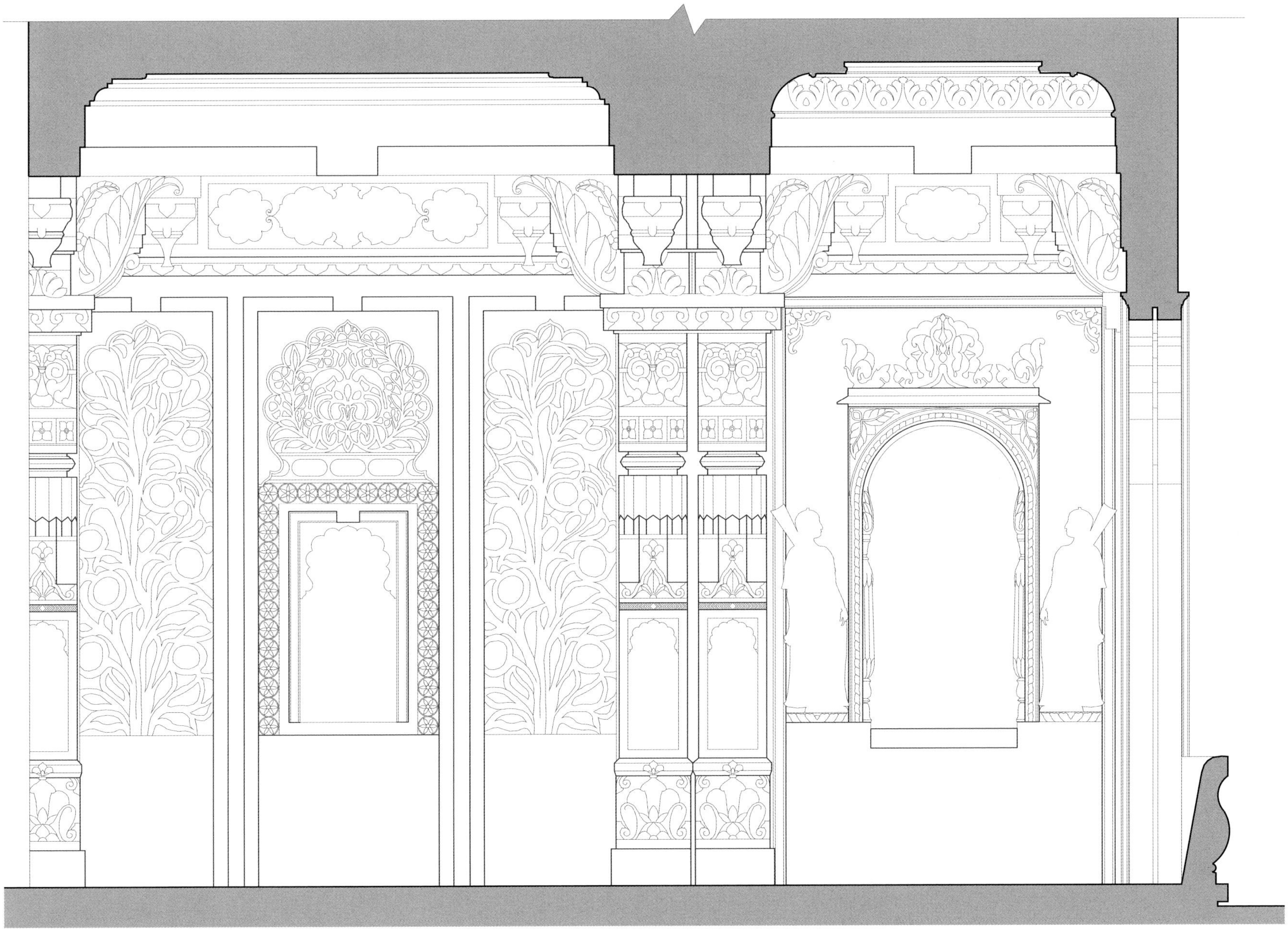

Elevation of spaces around Rai Angan

Kishan Vilas; the northern wing of the Badi Chitrashali courtyard was renovated by Maharana Bhim Singh as a memorial shrine dedicated to his sixteen year old daughter, Krishna Kumari, who poisoned herself to save her family from complications caused by her marriage alliance. The small room, the Vani Vilas was used by the scholar Shymaldas. Madan Vilas, the southern wing, built by Maharana Bhim Singh, was originally a verandah space similar to the Kishan Vilas, with stylistic changes in the form of cusped arched added in this phase. There were small scale interventions in the courtyard, with the change in flooring pattern in the central courtyard in the 20th century, possibly during Fateh Singh's reign.

Ornamentation of Mor Chowk

Mor Chowk is one of the courtyards that bear the mark of more than one ruler. Even though it was conceived in the 17th century during the reign of Maharana Karan Singh, it acquired its present identity only towards the end of this phase. The peacocks made of exquisitely inlaid glass mosaic work, carried out during the reign of Maharana Sajjan Singh, are considered masterpieces of great skill and artistry of the time and remain as some of the highly appreciated features in the palace.

The Swarup Vilas is a verandah with level with the east face of the Mor Chowk. This space, along with Surya Prakash was built by Maharana Swarup Singh as an enclosed gallery on the first floor of the Swarup Vilas with a series of cusped arches overlooking the Manek Chowk.The gallery linked the Bhim Vilas with Pitam Niwas.

The west wing comprised of a blank wall with a passage behind built in the early 20th century to

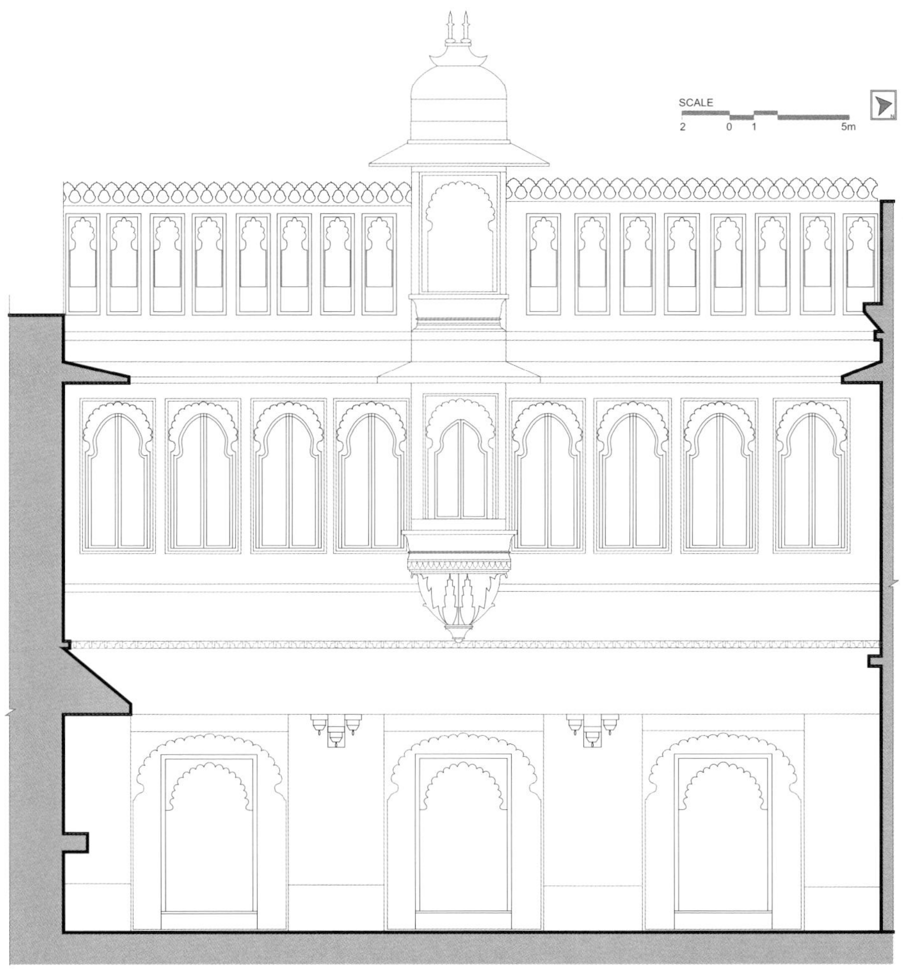

North Elevation of Mor Chowk

Above: Maharana Fateh Singh of Udaipur in durbar at Mor Chowk, The City Palace, UdaipurLeft to right standing:Pyarchand Mehta Dodiwalla; Bakhtawar Singh Sahiwala (with Mor Chhal); Jagnath Dhikadiya (with Mor Chhal) Left to right seated: Sambhunath Purohit, Chawand Rawat Guman Singh, Karohi Baba Bajai Singh, Sardargarh Thakur Manohar Singh, (behind the bolster) Sardar Bishan Singh, Maharana Fateh Singh, (behind the bolster) Fateh Lal Mehta, Rai Mehta Panna Lal, Gaddi walla Amar Singh, Maharaj Jai Singh,1884-1890, Acc. No: 2008.06.0470

allow an internal linkage with the Zenana Mahal. The small and increased number of openings with multifoliated cusped arches in both galleries varies slightly in style and scale but both are typical of the architectural style developed by Maharana Swarup Singh in the 19th century. Even the roof of the passage crowned by a series of close oblong *chatris* is unique to this period.

Bhim Vilas was renovated by Maharana Bhim Singh in the 19th century for his own use. 19th century building crafts of Mewar such as mirror work and intricately carved ivory doors can be found in Moti Mahal. Even the stone columns are covered with glass inlay work. The cusped arches are almost semicircular, as found in the 19th century, Mewar British phase. The paintings in Bhim Vilas are in bright colors of the Nathdwara Pichwai style, similar to what was executed in the Chitram ki Burj and depict the varied moods of Lord Krishna.

The first floor of the southern wing of Mor Chowk above Surya Chopad, called Pitam Niwas, was built as an enclosed space with cusped arches, in the period of Maharana Bhim Singh. It was used as an enclosed living space by the Maharana and has a lift from the ground floor that was a later intervention by Maharana Bhupal Singh. The space towards the north, provided with small cusped arched openings and windows with wooden blinds was used by the ladies of the royal family to view performances/events happening in Mor Chowk. Additionally, Manek Mahal which was originally built by Maharana Karan Singh was later decorated with glass inlay work by Maharana Swarup Singh in 19th century. He also closed a separate access to this space through a narrow ramp coming up from the Mardana *Deodhi* entrance.

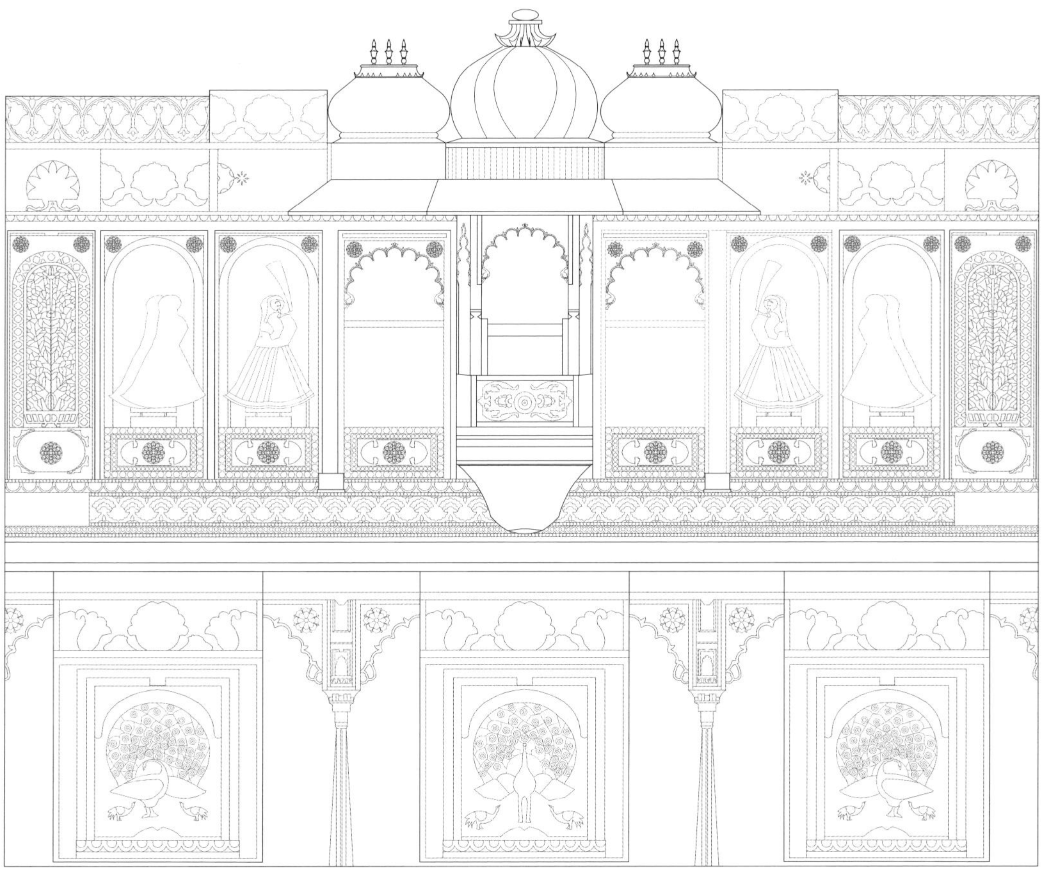

Facing Page: Present day view of Mor Chowk with glass inlay work.

Left: East Elevation of Mor Chowk (as received after photogrammetry by IIT Roorkee)

Above: 19th century Pichwai style painting in Bhim Vilas

Facing Page: Interiors of Bhim Vilas

महाराणाओं की पारम्परिक बैठक
TRADITIONAL SITTING
ARRANGEMENT FOR MAHARANAS

Zenana: Bhupal Vilas and Bhupal Prakash

The Zenana was also modified significantly in this phase, beginning with Zenana Deodhi, which showed a change in the opening archway. Wall Paintings and a *chatri* were also added in this phase. Pitambar Rai Mandir which was probably a part of the open space in front of Bhandar Chowk was walled off by Maharana Swarup Singh in 19th century to create its own separate courtyard. The earliest temple in this complex is Bannath ji Ka Mandir followed by Pitamber Rai ka Mandir.

In the early 19th century Maharana Bhim Singh started using the courtyard for the worship of Ban Mata during the Navratri festival that involved the ritual of sacrificing goats before the goddess. This practice continued till the late 20th century. The 20th century addition of a block on the southern portion changed the original shape of the courtyard. The staircase on the north east and upper floors is also a later addition. Within Amar Mahal, Maharana Bhim Singh placed the deity of Ban Mata in the front room. Toward the west and south ends of Amar Mahal, connecting spaces between the upper floor of the palace and that of the Zenana block were made by Maharana Fateh Singh to accommodate his son, Bhupal Singh. These spaces were known as Bhupal Prakash and Bhupal Vilas. These blocks also linked the Amar Mahal with the rest of the Zenana block. Bhupal Vilas was created on the southern end of Bhandar Chowk with the first floor as the living space for the 3rd queen of Maharana

View of Amar Mahal Chowk, The City Palace, Udaipur with presents being received from Bikaner, 1965-1970 CE, Acc. No: 2009.09.0087-00009

Maharana Bhupal Singh of Udaipur at private prayer. 1940-1950, Acc. No: 2008.06.0446

Bhupal Singh. It also linked the upper floor of Amar Mahal which was converted into Sarbat Vilas and Brij Vilas as living spaces for the royal queen.

The structure, made in stone and lime is reflective of new architectural styles of the period having high ceiling with girders, openings with ventilators and interiors with chandeliers, lights and wall paintings representative of early 20th century interiors.

The north and west wings show the maximum amount of interventions in this phase, with additions to the upper floors, most significant among them being the addition of floors and interiors spaces by Maharana Fateh Singh. In the north wing, the domes above the ground floor were removed to make space for two additional storeys. The Bhupal Prakash was another new block specially built by Maharana Fateh Singh for his son's second queen. This was created on the second floor of the western wing of Zenana Mahal. A special lift was installed on the northwest corner of Lakshmi Chowk to access the second floor as Maharana Bhupal Singh was suffering from health problems.

This facade of Zenana Mahal clearly shows the second floor as distinctly different with a greater height, semicircular openings within the cusped relief work and ventilators with *jaali*. The lakeside facade shows projected floor on small brackets with curved, floral motifs showing the change in architectural style. The inner spaces are hall like and much bigger than the lower floors. The interiors have semicircular door and colored glasses on ventilators of each door. In one case, there is even a painted false door to create symmetry in the interiors. It has similar decor as Bhupal Vilas with high ceilings, coloured walls and chandeliers.

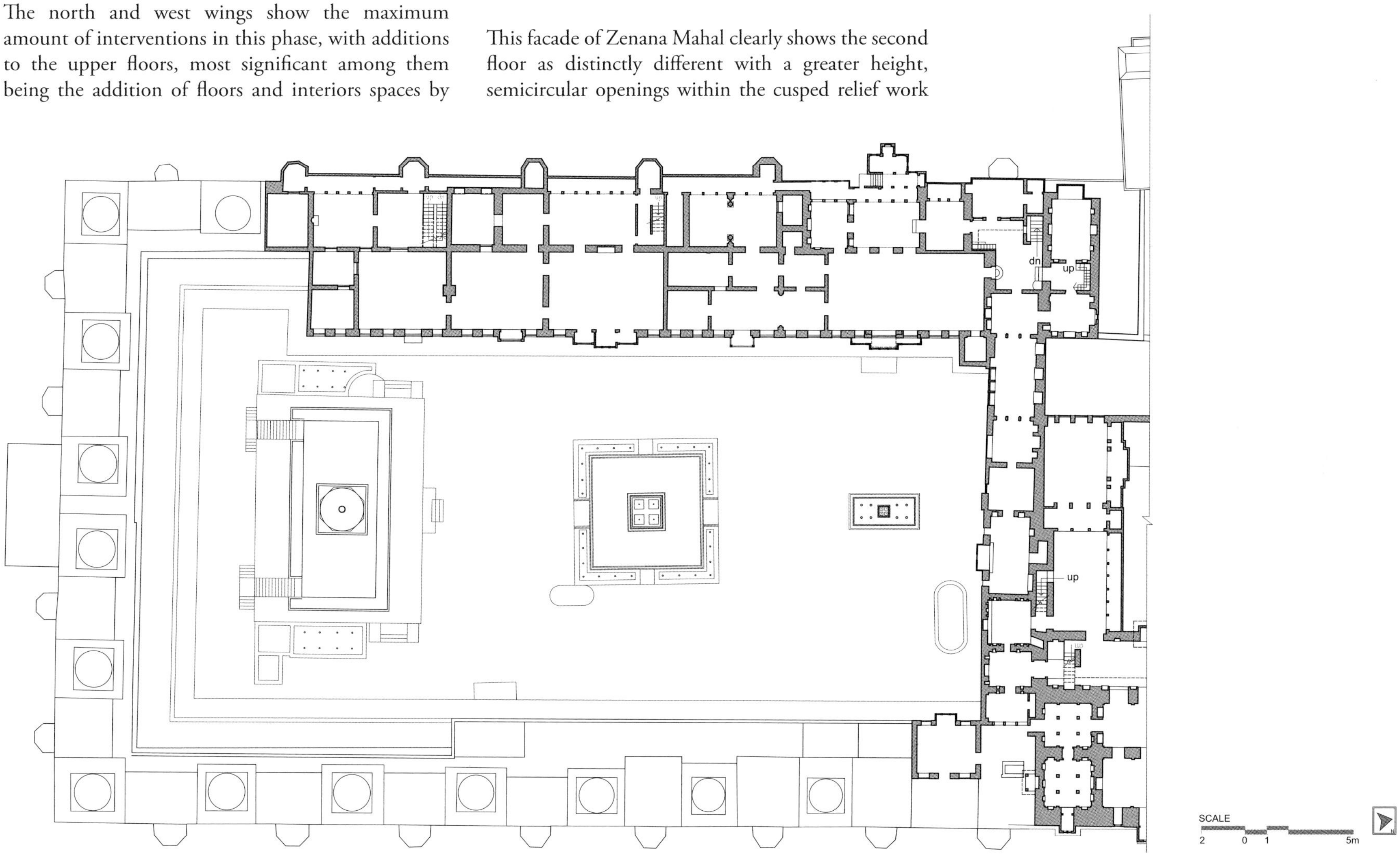

Plan of second level of Zenana Mahal

Peripheral Areas

The Badi Pol Chatris were modified in the 19th century, with the addition of *kullar* (small clay tubes) made locally to the cusped arches, giving the impression of a *jaali* from a distance. One opening was left with an entrance door in each of the *chatris*. Some of the lower arches were completely walled off.

The *Kothar*, which had served as the central storage area for most of the palace, as can be seen in numerous paintings depicting the areas was modified in the 1850s during the reign of Maharana Swarup Singh. The surrounding chambers were demolished to provide space for Khush Mahal, which was a new palace, constructed around two central courtyards and changed the skyline, and built with minimal ornamentation.

Tripoliya which had been constructed by Maharana Sangram Singh II in the early 18th century was modified, through the addition of another storey above the gateway. This storey, known as Hawa Mahal, owing to the addition of delicately carved screens shows the synthesis of three styles, the typical Mewar architectural features with Mughal *jaalis* and more colonial period floral motifs showing the British influence in the 19th century. The cusped arch opening, which was evolving from a bracketed arch in the previous phase was further refined in Hawa Mahal, with no gap in the centre, as observed in all openings of this period.

The western wing of Manek Chowk which comprised of Naharon ka Darikahana which was the earliest structure in front of Salehkhana was extended by the addition of Naginabadi Ka Darikhana in front of Sabha Shiromani created by Maharana Bhim Singh by converting an earlier garden into terrace space. This space would come to be an instrumental part of the annual Ashwa Pujan festivities which continue to this day. The Palkikhana, which was created in the 18th century by Maharana Sangram Singh II was also modified in this phase. An upper floor, known as the Ganesh Mandir with Lord Ganesha's idol was added in the 19th century by Maharana Swarup Singh.

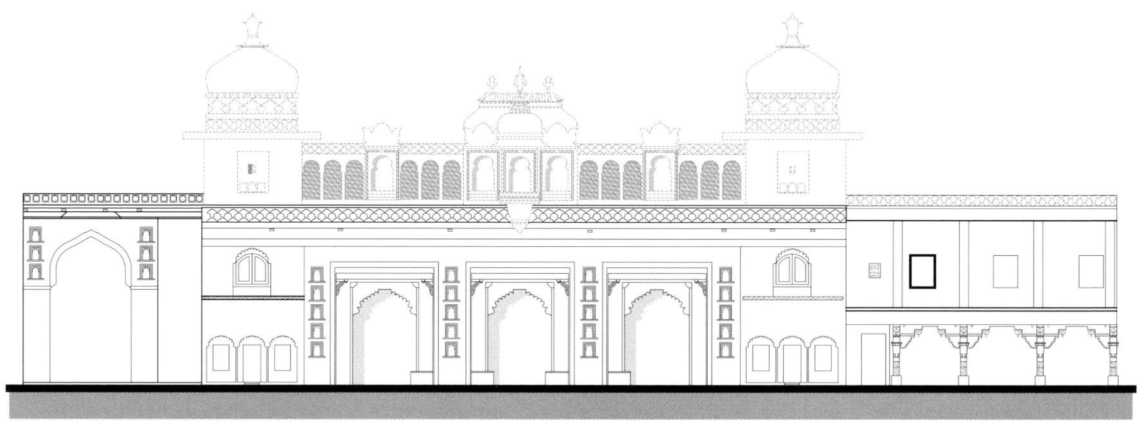

Above: South elevation of Tripoliya gate

Facing Page: The Manek Chowk, 1825–1905 CE, Acc No. 2009.10.0139-00046_R

New Structures

Shambhu Niwas, Shiv Niwas and Fateh Prakash were the three main palace structures which were built in this period. These three structures were designed as independent residences and guest-houses and thus their connection to the rest of the City Palace was also minimal. The technology, planning and ornamentation of the interiors as well as the exterior gardens show a dramatic evolution of style and scale. These palace areas are maintained today as private properties of Shriji Arvind Singh Mewar; Shambhu Niwas as a private residence and Shiv Niwas and Fateh Prakash as heritage hotels of the Historic Resort Hotels Group of Hotels. Khush Mahal which also dates to this period is located at the western edge of the palace, and bears stronger connection with the rest of the City Palace through Ganesh Chowk.

ABOVE: View of Shambhu Niwas Palace, Udaipur, 1895–1905, Acc. No: 2009.10.0139-00038
FACING PAGE: View of Fateh Prakash Palace, Udaipur, from Lake Pichola

Jacqueline Kennedy, wife of President John F. Kennedy of USA, with His Highness Maharana Bhagwat Singh Mewar of Udaipur during her visit to Udaipur on meeting the nobles of Mewar.
Photographer: K. L. Syed & Co.
16th March 1962
Acc. No. 2009.10.0180-00063

Princely India, Democracy and Institutionalisation

Post-Independence Mewar

This phase of development in the City Palace marks a paradigm shift in the use and significance of the site, and is characterised less by the changes to its built fabric and mostly recognised for several pioneering initiatives that have been put in place within its confines. Beginning with the reign of Maharana Bhupal Singh (r. 1930-1955 AD) up to the custodianship of Shriji Arvind Singh Mewar, this phase is noted for the realisation of Maharana Mewar Foundation (now Maharana of Mewar Charitable Foundation) as a charitable trust responsible for most parts of the City Palace. The City Palace was used as the royal residence until 1955. In 1971, after the abolition of the Privy Purse by the Government of India, royal families were denied their titles and major parts of their properties, except what was used as their private residence. The City Palace was transferred to the state government for a short period from 1955 to 1969; during this time the palace spaces were being used as government offices. Finally, Bhagwat Singh Mewar established the charitable trust to take care of the City Palace. After 1969, the City Palace was handed over to the Maharana of Mewar Charitable Foundation and converted into a museum.

Mewar as Part of Rajasthan

Maharana Fateh Singh was succeeded by his son Bhupal Singh, who was disabled for life and confined to a wheelchair after a debilitating illness. His father had therefore gone to great lengths to make the palace accommodations suitable. However, despite his physical frailties, Bhupal Singh's acumen as a ruler was as stellar as his father. Maharana Bhupal Singh ascended the throne at an extremely tumultuous time in the whole of India, not just Mewar. Through the intervention of the British, he had been vested with ruling powers since 1921, but due to the extent of popularity of his father, these powers were restricted till he was formally announced as the successor following Maharana Fateh Singh's death. During his reign, the campaign for reforms in education, health, legislation and transport, initiated by his father, was taken forward. This ensured that by the time Mewar was absorbed into the newly formed state of Rajasthan, it had made significant strides in both agriculture and industry. Various other public amenities were also improved during this phase. Hospitals and various medical facilities were introduced across the state and fresh impetus was given to higher education.

However, the overall political climate of India was in turmoil. The Satyagraha movement had strengthened in the entire country, and Udaipur was no different. These developments led to the formulation of the *Udaipur City Municipal Act*, 1945. With India's independence fast becoming a reality, several schemes for the merger of different Princely States were put forth, with Mewar being courted by different factions. On June 3, 1947 the British Government announced that it would transfer power to representatives of India and Pakistan on August 15, 1947. The Indian states had the option of acceding to either India or Pakistan, or of remaining independent. The Maharana of Mewar opted to sign the *Instrument of Accession* to India. Post-Independence was an equally turbulent period for Mewar as it was for the rest of the country. The Ministry of States in India declared that only viable Princely States would be allowed to maintain their identity. At this point, the Maharana opted to merge Mewar in the new state, and in April 1948, Mewar State joined the newly formed Union of Rajasthan.

Guest with Maharana Bhupal Singh of Udaipur at the wedding of Maharaj Kumar Bhagwat Singh of Udaipur, February 1940 CE, Acc. No: 2009.10.0193-00015

Maharana Bhupal Singh
AD 1930-1955

Maharana Bhagwat Singh
AD 1955-1984

Shriji Arvind Singh Mewar
AD 1984

Since once again, Maharana Bhupal Singh did not have a natural born heir, he adopted his great nephew Bhagwat Singh to succeed him. Faced with a dramatic change in status, both politically and financially, Maharana Bhagwat Singh was quick to adapt and maintain his position as a respected figure in Udaipur. Even though he no longer had a kingdom to rule after Independence and merger, Bhagwat Singh Mewar continued the religious observance of his ancestors as the custodian of Lord Eklingji. He found a continual need to adjust his thinking to the many changes that were occurring both at home and abroad. In 1971, the Privy Purse was abolished, which was a further financial blow to Bhagwat Singh.

His privileges and allowances ceased. Suddenly, he had to find an income, in part to maintain the many large palaces, since every one of them now was a taxable asset, liable to estate duty. Being a canny businessman, he seized the opportunity to convert several of his properties into luxury hotels and tourist destinations, an initiative that marks the beginning of heritage tourism in India. While this initiative was successful as a strategy for sustaining most of the palaces around the site, the historical City Palace posed to be a monumental task. Given its considerable age, it was in need of extensive repairs and the costs of maintaining it were formidable. Disheartened, Bhagwat Singh handed over the palace to the Rajasthan government with the hope that it would be restored and reused in an appropriate manner. Unfortunately due to a shortage of funds, the state government began using the spaces as government offices and the cycle of neglect continued in this manner.

Pained by the misuse and neglect of the City Palace, Bhagwat Singh persuaded the government to return the palace and began the restoration himself. Meanwhile, he had established a charitable trust, the Maharana Mewar Foundation, as a means to achieve the objectives of preserving the age-old traditions and obligations of the institution of Maharana. Primarily, the foundation's main purpose was to redevelop the main portions of the City Palace as a grand public museum of Mewar's history. Ongoing funding would come from accruing interest on the original investment and from entrance fee to the museum. The money earned from this foundation was to devolve to social welfare and education, and run the City Palace. Although Bhagwat Singh's lifestyle had changed from inherited sovereignty to businessman, he was determined not to forego the charter handed to his dynasty's founder, Bappa Rawal, part of which was to care for the welfare of his subjects in the name of Lord Eklingji. The mere fact that legally he no longer had any subjects as such was of no import. He utilised the income earned by the original Maharana Mewar Foundation to set up several subsidiary trusts for social welfare, education, religious and charitable purposes for the community.

Mayra party from Auwa at the wedding of Maharaj Kumar Bhagwat Singh in presence of Maharana Bhupal Singh of Udaipur at Mor Chowk, The City Palace, Udaipur. February 1940 CE, Acc. No: 2009.10.0193-00016

School children of Maharana Mewar Public School, Udaipur performing at an event organised by Maharana of Mewar Charitable Foundation

The City Palace as an Institution

The City Palace Museum and its collections celebrated over 1400 years of history of the Mewar dynasty and its attendant material culture. To inspire future generations, the Maharana of Mewar Charitable Foundation inaugurated a series of annual awards in order to recognise the achievement of individuals for services rendered to society and encouraging people's contribution towards Udaipur and Mewar. The fields of awards included art, music, dance, journalism, historical research, education and bravery in the course of duty. These awards are now internationally famous. Bhagwat Singh made a considerable financial donation to get the foundation to function. In 1972, an outpatients' dispensary was opened within the City Palace. Two years later, the Vidyadan Trust set up the Maharana Mewar Public School and a students' hostel. The old staff quarters, barracks, storerooms and stables of the City Palace were adapted for these new facilities, which are running successfully until today. A well-stocked library was established in the City Palace for students interested in historical research.

Maharana Mewar Special Library interior

There were few architectural interventions that have been made in this phase. Since part of the City Palace was converted to a museum, the once private spaces now had to address requirements of the general public; thus visitor facilities such as toilets, drinking water, resting benches, food were incorporated along with tourism related trade and commerce.

The long standing tradition of Mewar is retained in the continuity of the festive celebrations in Manek Chowk, headed by the royal family of Mewar and organised by the Maharana of Mewar Charitable Foundation. New events such as the Maharana Mewar Foundation Annual Awards have been introduced keeping in tune with changing times.

By the mid-20th century, the City Palace had become an ageing relic of a long and illustrious history. The conversion of the palace into a public museum not only ensured its long term longevity and relevance, it also highlights a series of glorious architectural and artistic achievements. Within the City Palace, visitor facilities, landscape furniture, shops and various other amenities were added.

Around 1974, a stage and open air stepped gallery was built in the Kothar area for the Maharana Mewar Public School by Maharana Bhagwat Singh. Presently referred to as the stadium, it is used by the children of Maharana Mewar Public School and Palace security guards for regular play as well as for special celebrations on occasions such as the Republic Day, Independence Day as well as other sports activities. Besides, it acts as the only access to the staff quarters located on the western side of this area.

Despite the fact that kingship is no longer recognised by the country's legal system, within Mewar, the continuation of the idea of custodianship is still alive and flourishing. This commitment to custodianship transcends political boundaries of kingship and democracy. It is further reinforced in the celebration of the annual regal festivals by the foundation and in the continuity of traditional processes of restoration applied at the City Palace.

Above: View of Rai Angan and Khasa Rasoda

Right: View of Manek Chowk during the Maharana Mewar Foundation Annual Award Distribution Ceremony.

Conservation and Adaptations

Background

The Maharana of Mewar Charitable Foundation (MMCF), Udaipur, was instituted by Maharana Bhagwat Singh Mewar in 1969, to which he donated a significant area of the City Palace and a sizeable financial contribution. The foundation was to enable practical and sustained use of the various palace structures, and at the same time serve as the seat of time honoured and cherished traditions of Mewar, maintaining the continuity of the custodianship by the royal family. The present Chairman and Managing Trustee of MMCF and the 76th Custodian of the House of Mewar, Shriji Arvind Singh Mewar, has taken forth his father's vision and the MMCF is committed to the long-term conservation and maintenance of the City Palace, Udaipur. The foundation utilises its resources in maintenance of the City Palace along with other philanthropic activities. The City Palace Museum, the Maharana Mewar Special Library, the Maharana Mewar Research Institute, the publications division and the educational institutes are some of the key projects within the City Palace being managed and developed by the foundation. From 1969-2004, MMCF had self-financed all conservation works in the City Palace.

In 2004, it was realised that though the foundation generated enough resources for regular maintenance of the City Palace, it still required substantial funds for developing a comprehensive conservation plan that could systematically prioritise conservation activities for the palace. Considering the vastness of this historic complex, the foundation requires matching funds and since 2005, it has collaborated with national and international grant makers for this purpose. As the first seminal step towards consolidating documentation, analysis and planning approaches for the City Palace, the preparation of the Conservation Master Plan was undertaken from 2005–2009, through grants awarded by the Getty Foundation in Los Angeles for assistance in architectural conservation of the palace. The implementation of this plan is an ongoing process since 2007, in phases, as per availability of funds. The most recent phase (2011–2016) involves the implementation of the Use and Interpretation Plan, setting up of the various museum galleries funded through grants from the Ministry of Culture, Government of India.

Preparing the Conservation Plan

The Conservation Master Plan for the City Palace has been prepared after an elaborate process of research, inquiry and investigations into the site's historical, architectural, social, political and environmental background as well an analysis of current issues and opportunities. A multidisciplinary team of architectural conservators, environmentalists, architects, material and art conservators, community planners and professionals in heritage tourism were involved in developing a framework. The plan was prepared by Development and Research Organisation for Nature, Arts and Heritage (DRONAH). Various participatory programs and workshops undertaken with organisations such as the National Museum at New Delhi, UNESCO India, Birla Institute of Technology at Ranchi, TVB School of Habitat Studies at New Delhi and Indian National Trust for Art and Cultural Heritage (INTACH) Udaipur Chapter were instrumental in preparation of the plan.

Framing the plans in coherence with policies, strategies and framework outlined by the Conservation Master Plan took place in two phases, with supporting training and workshops under each phase. The first phase (November 2005 – July 2007) encompassed preparation of a primary plan, namely the Conservation Master Plan for the site (completed in July 2009) along with executing a few identified emergency works. Under the second phase (November 2008 – October 2009), secondary plans, namely the Environment Management Plan, Interpretation and Use Plan, Lighting Plan and Risk Management Plan were prepared, with an intermediate level Cultural Heritage Tourism Plan that links with all primary and secondary plans and external framework affecting the site.

As part of the process, detailed archival research of the daily palace records known as *bahidas* and *ekantars* dating back to the 18th century was undertaken, along with a study of the various paintings and murals within the City Palace which dated to various phases of evolution of the structures, going back to the 18th century. The architectural spaces, styles, structural innovations, planning principles, use patterns and layers of interventions for each phase were identified based on the archives, visual analysis and through comparisons with other structures in the Mewar region. The different courtyards and their landscapes were analysed and recorded for the

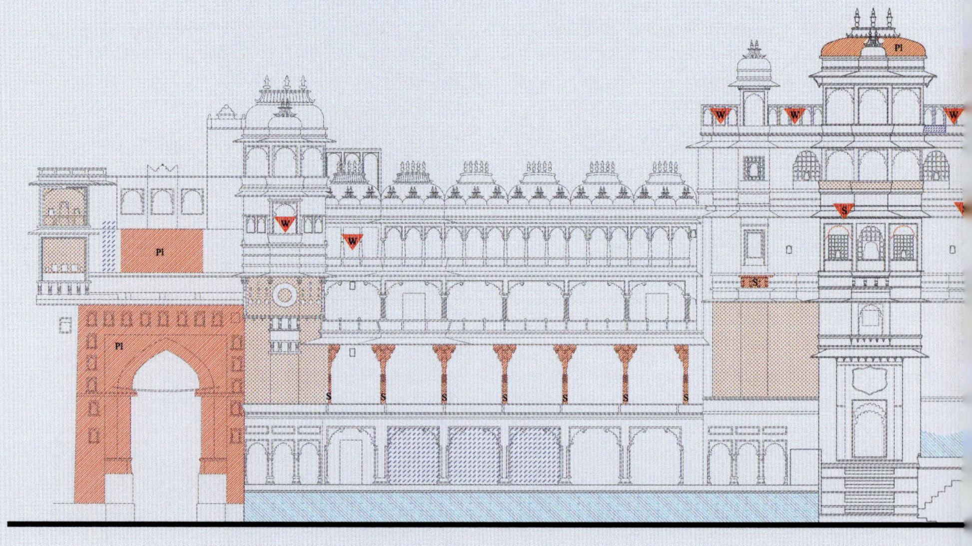

Above: Photogrammetry image of City Palace

Right: Typical condtion assessment image for Manek Chowk undertaken in 2005

built-open relationships within the palace. Additionally, rituals, festivals and oral traditions were recorded in detail through texts, paintings and interviews.

One of the key achievements of the first phase of planning was the compilation of an accurate set of documentation drawings for the palace, based on extensive topographical surveys and photogrammetry. The focus of this stage was on a multi-disciplinary approach to planning, with specific technical inputs from the various consultants. There were formal meetings to discuss conflicts and issues that came forth during the interim reports. Pilot projects and activities were also undertaken in this stage to establish certain frameworks for conservation within the palace.

In continuation to the work undertaken in the first phase of planning, a second phase of planning and implementation commenced under the Getty Planning Grant in 2008. The goals of this phase were primarily to support the objectives of the plan for the City Palace by completing all secondary plans identified. This included proposals outlining an interpretation and use strategy, an environment and landscape plan and a comprehensive risk management strategy that could be integrated with the overall conservation of the palace. The vision for the palace needed to be translated into specific policies and interventions and all activities on the site needed to respond to its unique cultural significance enriching the site and its message to the visitors.

The work on the projects began in November 2008 beginning with the preparation of the secondary plans as identified in the Conservation Master Plan. A six-month training programme was also started at this point, with the setting up of a special architectural cell in the Heritage Division of MMCF as a capacity building endeavour. The secondary plans were aligned to the master plan and technical drawings were prepared for conservation and landscape proposals. Detailed specifications and budgets were drawn up based on plans and drawings and finally the master plan was updated as a culmination of the second phase.

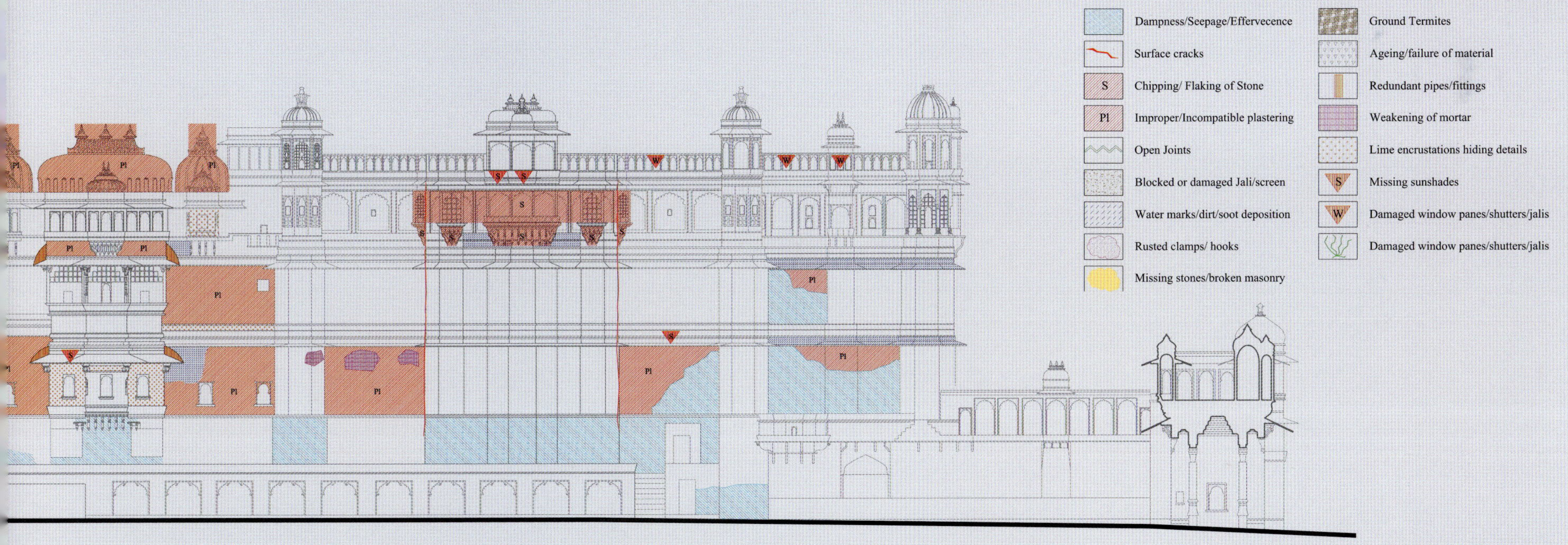

Approach for Living Heritage

The Conservation Master Plan is a dynamic document that is reviewed and updated as per implementation of various phases of the plan and site situations. The overarching mission of the plan is to acknowledge the tradition of custodianship and its role in conservation of the City Palace as well as enhance its cultural significance and integrate sustainability into decision making at all levels. The vision for the City Palace at Udaipur has been summarised as:

> "The living heritage of Eternal Mewar shall continue to reverberate dynamically through the multifaceted City Palace by conserving its past and integrating the evolving needs of the people in a manner that accrues environmental, social and economic benefits for its future."

A few of the primary objectives of the plan are to serve as a ready reference for the custodians of the City Palace to guide any decision ranging from the day to day maintenance to long term development of the site as well as ensure that current and future activities on the site further enhance the cultural significance and enrich the site experience for locals and visitors. The plan serves as a benchmark document for conservation sites in India and the world and sets an example of how a value based approach and process oriented planning can assist in conserving living heritage sites.

The Conservation Master Plan has a dual purpose; while it primarily addresses the site specifics for the realisation of the identified vision and objectives, it also aims to serve as a model in heritage management and conservation in the wider context of evolving conservation discipline nationally and internationally. This unique site is envisioned as an educational resource where implementation of this plan will not only cater to immediate conservation needs of the site but further serve as a laboratory for onsite training programs and promoting academic dialogue and outreach initiatives. This plan aims to bring forth the Indian perspective of living heritage to international conservation arena. It is further supported within a framework of primary and secondary plans that have evolved as a response to identified threats, issues and opportunities for the site during the planning process.

The conservation philosophy for the City Palace, Udaipur goes beyond mere technical restoration, to encompass the social, cultural and the natural realms. It aims to conserve the built heritage in its entirety, along with its geographical and socio-cultural morphology. This conservation approach thus outlines conservation policies and prioritises conservation activities that preserve and improve identified values of the City Palace by addressing both its tangible and intangible heritage in totality that constitutes the living heritage. Conservation policies for the City Palace are based on thorough research and understanding of complicated historic and socio-cultural layers on the site and its present and future operational needs. Policies for built fabric focus on the authenticity of the historic fabric in the site specific context and material conservation needs based on the in-depth analysis of the historic layers. Appropriate environmental conservation guidelines are based on the symbiotic relationship between the built heritage and the natural setting of the lake and the ridge, thus addressing the environmental concerns regarding the natural setting. The City Palace is a living heritage site, an embodiment of the social and ritual traditions of Mewar region for centuries. Hence, conservation polices integrate the continuity of socio-cultural values to address the needs and aspirations of the local community to attain social sustenance.

The first step was an exhaustive research and documentation of the site that has since become a resource base for evolving the analysis and developing the plan, in addition to being a permanent documentation of the spaces, their usage and evolution. This was followed by comprehensive site surveys and a detailed analysis of the physical condition of the structures within the site to identify key issues and threats. The documentation phase was essential not only from the point of view of identifying various historic layers and determining the most effective conservation techniques but also informed the interpretation strategy of the palace as a whole and adaptive re-use of its various spaces. At every stage, decisions regarding the City Palace were taken collectively with the custodians, local residents and stakeholders of the palace, and through the inputs of various technical experts. This phase lead to the realisation that the basic philosophy guiding conservation works on site has to address the entire spectrum of significance, issues, and constraints as well as being grounded within the site's physical, social, environmental and economic context. This meant that in addition to taking into account national and international charters, existing statutory frameworks and contemporary debates in the conservation arena, the site's unique values and significance as well as traditional practices and beliefs associated with it would need to be considered.

ABOVE: Traditional process for grinding lime

LEFT: Ongoing conservation work inside Mor Chowk in 2004-2005

Conservation of the Palace Spaces

Perspective of the Custodians

Throughout the long and illustrious history of the City Palace, there exists a common thread of addition, reconstruction, repair and renewal. Various Maharanas over the centuries have undertaken ambitious campaigns of extending the City Palace, adding new layers to existing structures and repairing and maintaining the old, with a reverence that is still visible today. This continued patronage of the City Palace by the royal family for centuries has given it a unique complexity of architectural form, while ensuring its survival. This approach pre-dates the colonial period when conservation and restoration came to be recognised as formal and scientific methods to protect architectural heritage.

One can trace some of the first large scale 'restorations' undertaken by the royal family of Mewar back to the Mughal period, to the reign of Maharana Jagat Singh I who undertook the task of repairing Chittorgarh's decaying fortifications. His actions were in direct contravention to the treaty signed between the Maharanas of Udaipur and the Mughal Emperor. The restoration of Chittorgarh was to remain a subject of dissent over the following years, with Jagat Singh's successors, Maharana Raj Singh attempting to carry out extensive restorations to the fortifications and other structures. During the early 20th century, the issue of restoring Chittorgarh came up again, though in a different context, with the newly instituted Archaeological Survey of India disapproving of the way Maharana Bhupal Singh had undertaken repairing the Vijai Stambha 'in conflict with archaeological needs'. The Archaeological Survey's disapproval of the manner in which the royal family approached their heritage possibly marks one of the first debates surrounding conservation approaches in the Mewar region.

One can find several examples of Maharanas undertaking extensive repairs to the palace structures, and further adding layers of ornamentation to existing spaces, especially in the third and fourth phases of the palace's evolution. This spirit of preserving centuries old tradition while adding one's own identity to the City Palace persists even today. Shriji Arvind Singh Mewar has added his own unique expression to the palace, as can be seen in the Lakshmi Chowk, with the Millennium Dome added above the Chowmukha Pavilion, a structure that dates back to the reign of Maharana Sangram Singh II. At the same time, respect for one's predecessors is evident in his recent interventions to the Tripoliya; where the addition of three

ABOVE: The Millennium Dome added above the Chowmukha pavilion in the Lakshmi Chowk, The Zenana Mahal

FACING PAGE: A procession during the royal wedding in Moti Chowk

massive timber gateways has been carried out as homage to his ancestors under whose patronage the gateway was built.

The continued custodianship reflects the way the site was used, maintained or taken care of, using the best known contemporary approaches, as well as continuity of traditional processes. Some traditional craftsmen associated with the royal family have been retained over generations enabling this continuity. The traditions that were associated with the life of the royal family such as annual celebrations and regal festivals continue to have citizens' participation even today. The religious spot of Dhuni Mata, the point of origin of the City Palace, continues to be revered with the daily lighting of a lamp. The royal family has continued linkage with the site as both its patrons and its users. The temples within the complex are worshipped by the royal family even today and royal ceremonies are still carried out in the ritual courtyards of the palace.

This continuity value can be read and appreciated as the tradition and cultural association that had kept the City Palace intact till 2005, even in the absence of a formal conservation approach. The continuity of use and adaptations to suit the needs of the moment by the custodians has enabled sustainability of resources. What is exceptional in the palace is the 'process' that has evolved over generations around this unique site with continuous exchange and interactions of space, place and people, thereby becoming an established mode of practice. The plan making for the site records the dialogue between theory and practice on the site and negotiations between age old traditions and new concepts of conservation.

Dialogue with International Conventions

The City Palace presents some unique issues that the contemporary discipline of conservation needs to address. While theoretically, conservation of built heritage often rests on the revival and restoration of structures that are dilapidated or defunct, in India, and especially in the palace, the situation is dramatically different. The palace has been in continual use for centuries and patrons involved in its care have evolved indigenous methods and norms for its protection and survival. In such a scenario it is not enough to simply prescribe general conservation guidelines as per recently established Eurocentric norms. There is a need to balance the unique values of continuity and custodianship associated with the palace with internationally accepted approaches. This process has resulted in the Conservation Master Plan that is a dynamic document, that responds to the unique character of the City Palace and at the same time adheres to international standards of conservation.

Some of the key doctrinal texts that informed the plan included the *Australia ICOMOS Burra Charter* for it clarity in setting up a framework for assessing significance, an aspect crucial for a value based approach; the *Charter for the Conservation of Unprotected Architectural Heritage and Sites in India* (INTACH, 2004), for the specific definition of authenticity in the Indian context and for recognising the context of 'living heritage' applicable to the site and lastly, Principles for the *Conservation of Heritage sites in China* (Getty Conservation Institute, 2004) as a reference document in the Asian context and more specifically, for its content specification for a Conservation Master Plan. While these documents helped in developing a balanced and objective perspective for the City Palace, it was the exhaustive analysis of the significance and values associated with the site itself, including an understanding of the 'concept of custodianship' indigenous to Mewar that refined the planning approach and ensured that the master plan was a unique solution to a unique site, with a highly specific context.

During the first phase of the Getty funded project, a number of issues related to conflicting conservation approaches came forth. The major issues were addressed by establishing basic guidelines for conserving the built fabric. These included the guidelines for the use of non-traditional material and processes as a solution only in extreme scenarios when the damage had to be controlled immediately to save the structure. The removal of original building material was recommended only in special circumstances, such as in cases where the original material had outlived its function, or could not be retained due to extreme deterioration. At this point, several debates surrounded the issues of appropriateness of carrying out major restoration work, to achieve aesthetic unity. Traditionally, the City Palace had been renovated extensively under the care of various Maharanas, who carried out extensive repairs to the palace when required. The concept of minimal intervention and preserve as found were relatively new approaches, and their applicability in the context of the City Palace was questioned. Consequently, it was decided that major restoration work to the City Palace would be acceptable, provided sufficient evidence is available on site and no conjecture is involved, the craftsmanship has the ability to match the original quality of the palace, and that all materials are tested before application. Considering the existing availability of skilled craftsmen in building arts in Udaipur, major restoration is not only possible, but also encouraged as a means to preserve the living heritage of Udaipur city and enhance the continuity value of the City Palace.

However, caution in conservation is also essential, bearing in mind that a lot of the work in the City Palace is unique in its conception and execution and that any irreversible change to the historic fabric of the palace would result in a huge loss of significance. Hence, one of the first recommendations of the conservation approach has been that any process of restoration be documented at all stages and disseminated to the public. Any major restoration work of exceptional art work or building crafts dated to a much earlier period that would be impossible to reproduce with current craftsmen and materials should not be undertaken.

Formulating Sustainable and Ecological Approach

In the first phase of the project, the conservation process included regular maintenance work and emergency conservation work, which was identified during the documentation and assessment phase. Apart from these activities, a pilot project involving the conservation of one of the Badi Pol Chatris- the Naqqarkhana ki Chatri was also undertaken. The pilot project was taken as a means to establish onsite challenges, evaluate issues and reinforce conservation policies. During the onsite works that were carried out along with the preparation of the plan, a number of technical and social issues came forth. These issues had a direct impact on policy making. It was realised that the final decision should only be arrived at after a detailed condition assessment and exhaustive consultations with local craftsmen, experts and custodians.

Prior to the entire process of developing comprehensive conservation policies for the City Palace, there was little awareness regarding appropriate materials and technologies for conservation. Most of the recent repairs had been carried out in cement based mortars and plasters. The local work force was disengaged with traditional building practices and technologies that had existed in the region. However, a few elderly artisans employed in the palace for fine lime plastering and also some elderly masons in the city who were aware of traditional technologies were engaged. A local contractor already working in the palace possessing a basic knowledge of traditional techniques of building construction was identified. In addition, local members of his team gained knowledge and skills from the skilled elderly masons. All building materials were sourced locally.

Traditional process for grinding of lime

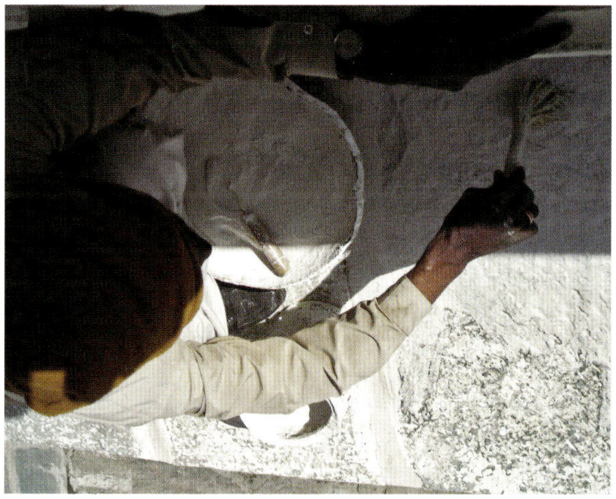

Right:

1. Raking out the aged plaster from within the joints in the sunshades
2. Filling of the joints with lime mortar
3. and 4. Applying of limewater over the surface of the sunshade
5. Levelling and applying the first layer plaster using lime and marble dust
6. Completion of the first layer of plaster

Facing Page: Removal of deteriorated plaster from the exterior surfaces of Baadi Mahal

Newly formulated policies for the palace were put to the test in 2006, while the plan was still in the process of being written. An exceptionally heavy monsoon season caused a considerable amount of damage to various structures within the palace. At this time, it became imperative to undertake conservation of several areas. The historic Paiga or stables area in Manek Chowk had suffered extensive damage due to rain, and the situation was in need of immediate emergency action. In this instance, a combination of chemical waterproofing and traditional lime work was used; chemical grouting ensured that maximum original fabric was retained and the traditional waterproofing was done as part of long term maintenance measures.

Wherever possible, traditional techniques were used for conservation, while maintaining the rigour demanded by international conservation standards. Thus, during the restoration of Baadi Mahal, one of the most significant of palace spaces, the physical damage was carefully documented in exhaustive detail, prior to carrying out any repairs. All cracks were carefully monitored using non-destructive techniques. The monitoring of cracks was conducted for an entire year revealing that there was no further increase in the cracks. Eventually, these cracks were filled with lime mortar. The lime plaster of several of the interior spaces was replaced and cornices and ornamental plaster work was restored. Within the interior spaces, such as Yash Mandir, the monsoon rains were posing a major structural threat to the decorative art work. In order to prevent further damage, lime terracing was re-laid in the traditional manner, and terracotta water spouts on the terrace that were broken or missing were replaced with matching spouts sourced from a nearby village.

A long term maintenance strategy was also established during this time. Maintenance activities in several areas of the City Palace set the standard for future approaches to maintenance and upkeep within the palace and helped establish various methodologies and procedures for common issues that recur in the palace.

One of the key pilot projects in the City Palace is the conservation of Nakkarkhana ki Chatri, one of the *chatris* of the Badi Pol, undertaken in 2006. The assessment of physical condition of the *chatris* was undertaken as part of a training workshop organised in collaboration with the TVB School of Habitat Studies, New Delhi. During the preliminary assessment, various issues to the masonry and structure were identified, including cracked beams, damaged *chajjas*, peeling plaster and finishes and ageing of the mortar. This project was an essential step to identify and address issues related to living heritage sites, such as conflicts between following of traditional processes and modern approaches.

The restoration work was started in December 2006 and was completed in July 2007, in a four stage process. The first stage was setting up a lime preparation mechanism that involved a traditional lime preparation method using *garhat* (a grinding stone driven by bullocks on a circular track) which was set up in one of the open areas. The second stage was cleaning, consolidation and replacement of damaged material. The debris from the site was cleared and the various additions, accretions and interventions on the chatri were carefully removed. This was followed by consolidation of the structure, which included pointing of stone masonry joints on all the surfaces with lime and marble dust mortar and stitching of cracks on beams and arches using lime and marble dust mortar. The existing, broken *kullar* or clay tube screens were replaced with matching clay tubes, and two doors were added to secure the structure from vandals and pests. As a means of consolidation, deteriorated plaster from external surfaces of the turret base was removed; joints were properly raked and re-pointed with matching lime mortar and finally lime plaster was applied in two layers. Subsequently, lime wash or *khamira* was applied to the clay tube screens, the infill walls, and the dome of the structure as a protective layer. Finally, the gold plated spire (*kalasha*) on top of the dome was cleaned, removed for gilding and replaced and the traditional drums called the *nakkaras* were also restored.

The restoration involved revival of the original use, but modified to adapt to the present day context. The original use of the Nakkarkhana ki Chatri was that of a drum house with the *nakkara* housed at the second level in the chatri. The use had been discontinued since Maharana Bhupal Singh's death in 1955. To revive the initial use of the *chatri*, the *nakkara* was restored and the ritual of beating the *nakkara* at specific times of the day was revived in July 2007. Due to the change in the cultural and political context, the ritual of announcements regarding arrival and departure of esteemed visitors has not been continued, but the announcement of time (three times during the day) as done traditionally, by the beating of *nakkara*

Above:

1. Yash Mandir terrace before the fresh terracing was done
2. Removing of the existing deteriorated and pulverised terracing
3. And 4. Preparing the mixture for the lime terracing, using organic additives
5. The first layer of lime terracing in process of application and manual consolidation
6. Consolidation of second layer of terracing using sticks and battons

has been revived. This use of *nakkarkhana* maintains the spirit of the place and is appropriate for the City Palace that now functions as a museum.

The continuity value identified in the master plan as the unique value of the City Palace was addressed by integrating the continuity of traditions and rituals such as the beating of the *nakkara* as well as encouraging traditional rituals observed in restoration practice such as the gilding of the finial and its worship before reinstallation. Throughout the conservation work, the significance of the structure in term of its aesthetic character was maintained by enhancing existing architectural elements such as the screens, cleaning of brackets, domes and arches. It was ensured that new interventions such as the clay tube screen at lower level and the metal grille door are in harmony with the existing structure in form, scale and proportion. The social value was enhanced by reviving the use of the *chatri* as a *nakkarkhana* for beating of drums. The restoration project though small in scale has had a long term policy impact. It serves as a model for the range of conservation works to be taken up for the entire City Palace and for other significant heritage within Udaipur. The

Above:

1. A mixture of crystallised asafoteida (*heeng*) paste and lime water was prepared
2. and 3. The roots of the plant were injected with this mixture
4. The plan wilted as a result of the organic weedicide used
5. Removal of tobacco stains using lime juice and nylon brushes

project is a step towards developing a sound policy for conservation practice in the Indian context by addressing local values and their conflict with 'authenticity' of the structure.

Since 2007, conservation work at the City Palace has received fresh impetus, and several spaces and structures within the museum have been conserved. The Ghadiyal ki Chatri and the Badi Pol were restored by 2009, based on the learning of the pilot project carried out at the Nakkarkhana ki Chatri. Various other initiatives have been undertaken both in the interior spaces and the courtyards. The various Pols or gateways that enclose different courtyards of the palace have been restored, namely Tripoliya, Toran Pol, Kothar Pol, Paiga Pol, Zenana Deodhi and Badi Zenana Deodhi. Three massive wooden gates were also added to the arched openings of the Tripoliya, by Shriji Arvind Singh Mewar in 2010. The exquisite murals on the ceiling of Toran Pol were also restored and re-painted by an expert local artist who was proficient in the painting style. The latest restoration work on Suraj Pol is being implemented in 2014

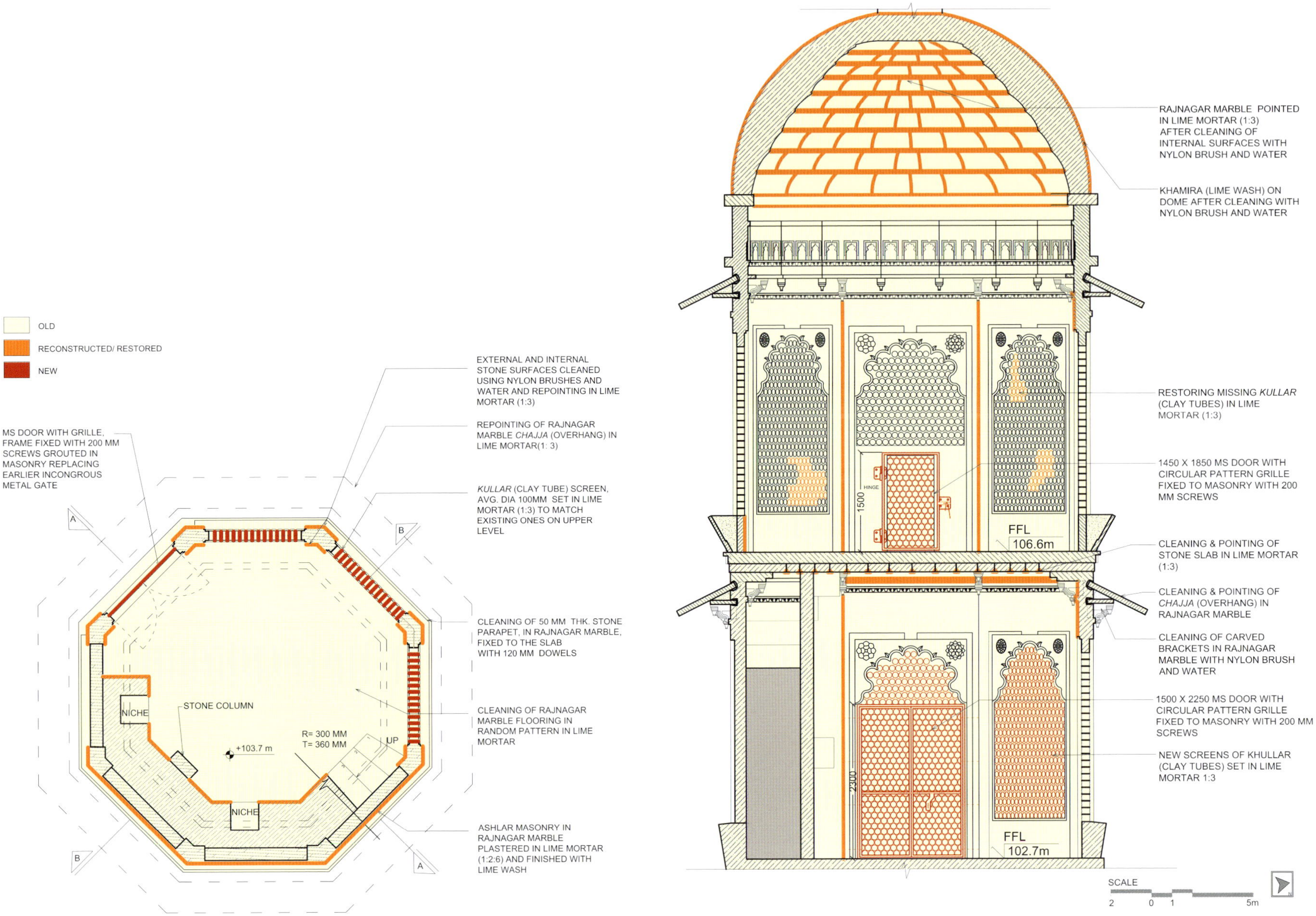

Detailed conservation drawings prepared for the Nakkarkhana ki Chatri

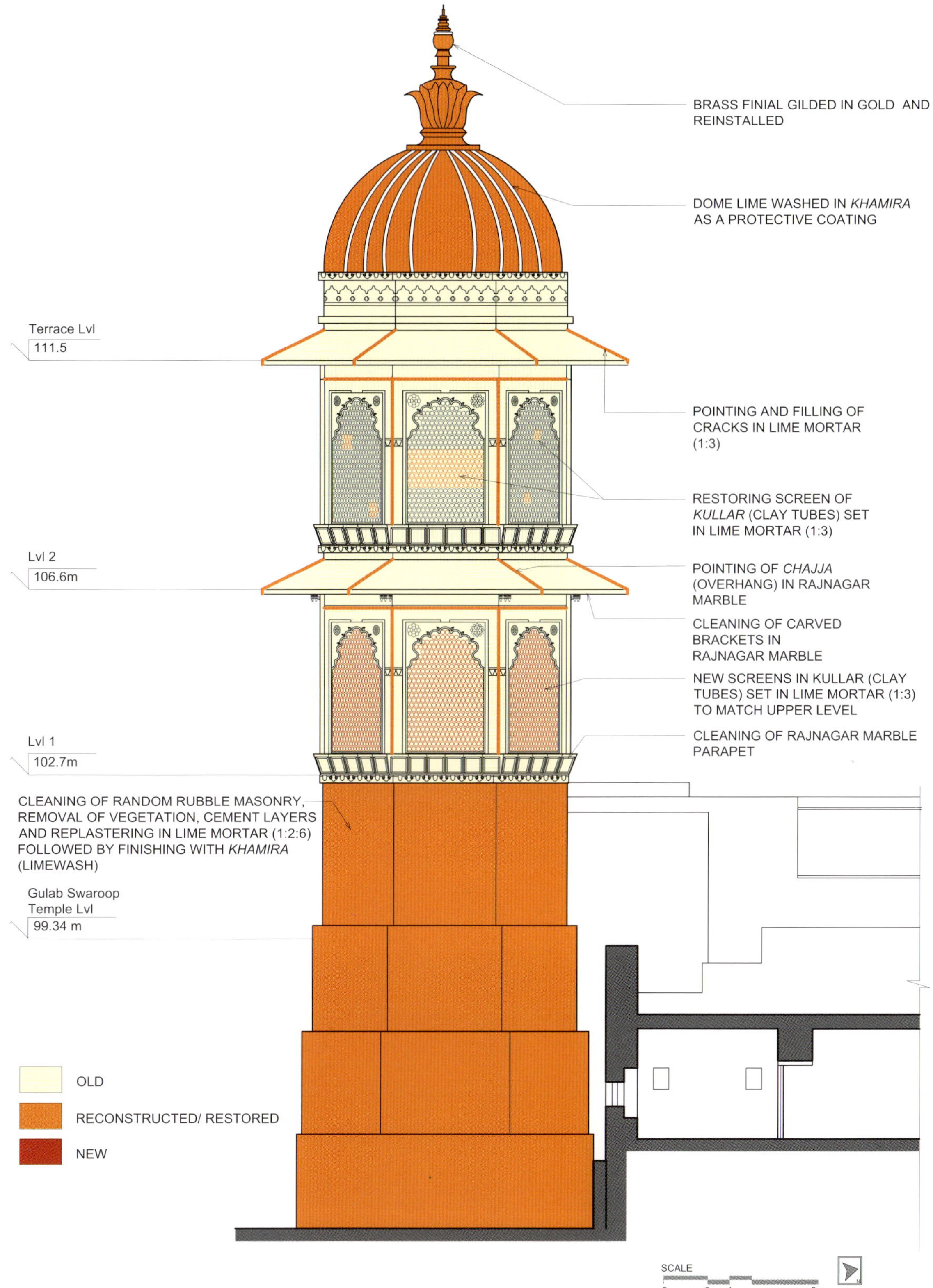

Detailed conservation drawings prepared for the Nakkarkhana ki Chatri

Above:

1. Scaffolding fixed on the exteriors of the Chatri
2. Temporary removal of the copper with gold polish spire on top of the dome, for cleaning and polishing
3. Cleaning of interior stone surfaces using nylon brushes and water

Right: Craftsmen carrying out art conservation in the ceilings of Toran Pol

Facing Page: The recently conserved Toran Pol

An account of Kuvar lal ji, Nakkarkhana Vadak, City Palace

Kuvar Lal belongs to a family that has been associated with the playing of nakkara and shehnai in the royal house of Mewar for many generations. He has continued the family tradition and plays the *nakkara* and *shehnai* at the palace. According to him, the *shehnai* was played three times in a day; the first time in the early morning hour, in the evening also known as naubat, and finally at night (9:00pm to 10:00 pm). The *nakkara* and *shehnai* was located on Suraj Pol but during the period of Maharana Bhagwat Singh, the *nakkara* and *shehnai* were shifted to Shambhu Niwas. Presently, *nakkara* and *shehnai* are located in the City Palace near the Hathi Agad. The *nakkara* was also played for greetings to other royal families and for special occasions and these *nakkaras* were located outside the Zenana Deodhi. The *nakkaras* were carried along with the procession of royal families on horseback. For the Ganguar processions as well as the Maharanas' processions the *nakkaras*, were carried on elephant.

Holika Dahan ceremony

City Palace as a Living Museum

Continuity and Adaptations

The City Palace has historically housed multiple functions and ceremonies as the royal residence and political headquarters of Mewar. Its various courtyards and smaller palace rooms have been used over centuries for a variety of functions, ranging from grand public courtyards such as Manek Chowk, to intimate leisure spaces such as Baadi Mahal. Several spaces have had a unique purpose and significance, such as the Dhuni Mata in Rai Angan or Pitamber Rai ji ka Mandir that are still some of the most sacred spaces within the palace. The multiplicity of use has continued since the institutionalisation of the palace and it currently accommodates several different activities, such as a public museum, research institute, traditional music foundation, offices and a dispensary while serving as a thoroughfare and access area to a few surrounding sites such as the heritage hotels, Maharana Mewar Public School and the government museum housed in Karan Mahal. At the same time, the City Palace continues to hold special significance for both its custodians and the local populace and many traditional festivals and rituals continue to be held in the spaces of the palace. The City Palace Museum is thus a 'living' museum, in that it is more than a static display of artefacts of an era gone by, rather, it is a constantly evolving space, that is physical evidence of a long cherished tradition of custodianship.

The core of the City Palace; Mardana Mahal and Zenana Mahal are spaces primarily designated for museum use. The museum was conceived as an in-house initiative of MMCF and though it functioned well for the last few decades, the spaces and galleries required re planning that integrated the recent historic research and findings about the site.

The City Palace is a landmark for the community as a symbol of Mewar culture as the seat of administration for 22 generations and is a symbol cultural integration of heritage with community for 'living' heritage within the Indian context. The previous custodians of Mewar have ensured that in addition to the site itself, the community, traditions, events and memories have been valued and passed on from one generation to the next. To maintain this value, a sensitive and holistic approach towards reuse and planning for the City Palace is of paramount importance. The site is already communicating a number of messages to the locals and visitors through its existing functions, festivals, events and programs such as the Sound and Light Show. The Interpretation and Use Plan thus integrates existing messages within its overall messages to respond to the wider context of Mewar.

In the context of Indian history and culture, several indigenous interpretative modes have existed for centuries. Within the specific regional context of Mewar, these can be identified as local story telling and narrations by poets, bards and chroniclers and should be treated as sources of information about the site. The local arts and crafts which have traditionally been used as a means of communication include storytelling, folk songs and dramas, dance, plays, skits and puppets. To maintain these indigenous methods as part of mainstream media for communication of the messages in the interpretation plan will be an additional challenge, but at the same time a unique opportunity to explore different forms of interpretation.

Significantly, the City Palace has the potential to be a museum comparable with current international norms for museum planning, research and collections management and exhibition design. The multifaceted use of the present site with the museum and offices of other organisations promoting art, archives, literature and music of Mewar can be integrated to present the site usage as a cohesive whole. Separate plans for the museum facilities and for the assessment, cataloguing, conservation and dissemination of the museum collections are prepared and are under implementation keeping in full view of its living heritage dimension.

Right: Facilities planning in the City Palace Museum

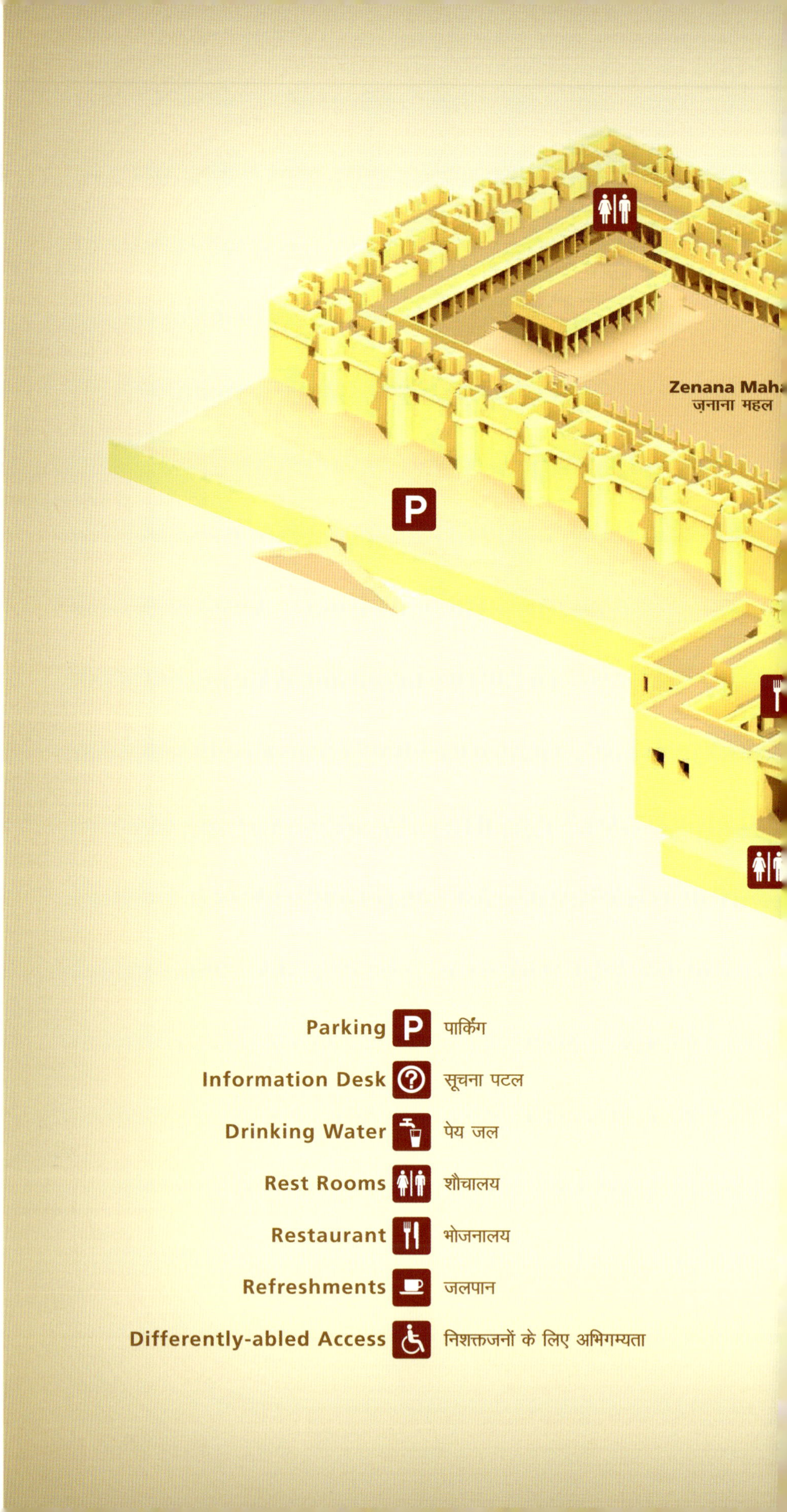

The City Palace Museum
सिटी पैलेस संग्रहालय

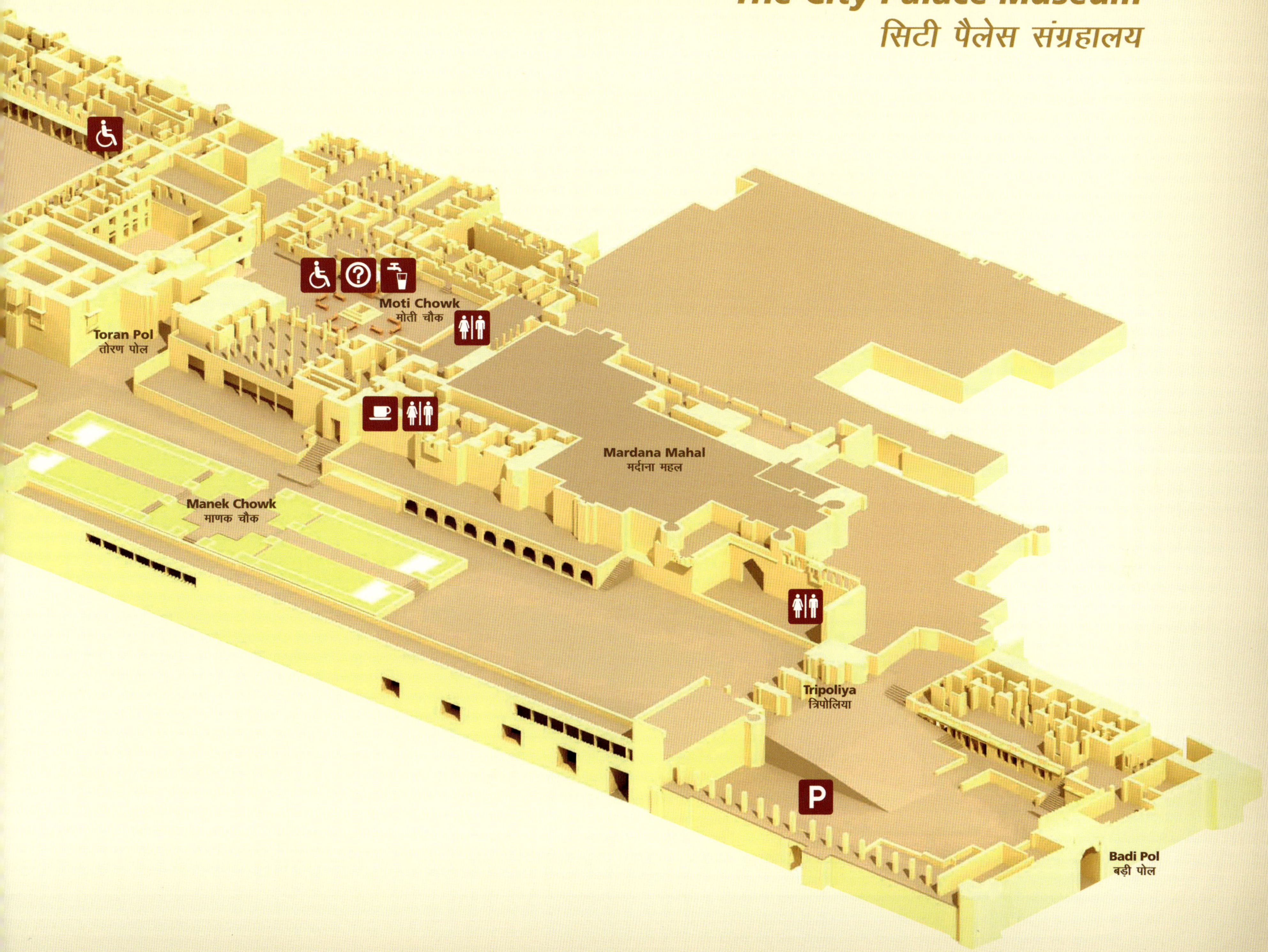

Historically, the spaces within the City Palace could be broadly classified as the public spaces and the outer courtyards, comprising of the two key spaces, Manek Chowk and Moti Chowk and the two distinct zones of the palace, Mardana Mahal and Zenana Mahal. Each set of spaces had further subdivisions in the form of courtyards and palace structures with varying uses and degrees of significance. When the palace spaces were converted into the City Palace Museum, individual galleries were based on three themes; the first being the palace spaces themselves, the second comprising of interpretation and story based galleries and the third theme comprising of collection and lifestyle galleries. The itinerary of the visitor has been designed so that through the outer courtyards, the visitor is directed into Mardana Mahal and a singular route takes him through various internal spaces to Zenana Mahal. Through the various spaces, one visits all the galleries.

The initial assessment of the City Palace in 2005-2006 brought forth some key issues which made it difficult for visitors to absorb the entire history and cultural significance of the site. Of these, the absence of explanatory signage at strategic locations and the lack of an orientation and interpretation centre were in need of urgent attention. Other issues included lack of effective communication regarding the significance of certain spaces within the palace. Poor presentation, lighting and a convoluted circulation route were some of the causes identified. Despite the fact that a number of separate displays attempted to depict some of the most iconic stories associated with the history of Mewar, the visitor was unable to piece together a coherent storyline by the end of his visit. In part, this is due to the overlapping circulation between different types of gallery spaces within a single visitor route.

The historic core of the City Palace no longer serves as the permanent residence of the royal family of Udaipur, since the residential spaces are now housed in the newer palace spaces. However, historic links to the spaces and the connections to the City Palace religious and ritual spaces remain powerful still. Hence, even though many of the palace spaces are now permanent galleries, various annual rituals, events and festivals are continually organised within the museum. For instance, the Lakshmi Chowk is still the space where royal weddings are held and the royal procession will enter through the Badi Pol, Tripoliya and Toran Pol. In addition to traditional activities, various new initiatives by the MMCF have been initiated to foster the relationship of the royal family with the local population in Udaipur. The City Palace is thus still evolving and growing as a space with new functions assigned to it in response to its evolving relationship between the custodians, visitors and locals.

Right: The setting for a wedding organised in Lakshmi Chowk, The Zenana Mahal

Museum Galleries and Public Spaces

The Ashwa Poojan Ceremony in Manek Chowk

The proposed interpretation and use plan of the City Palace has been based on a set of objectives which respond to the unique character and setting of the site. The objectives have been defined after a thorough analysis of the site challenges with response to policies framed in the Conservation Master Plan. One of the primary objectives identified for the City Palace Museum is to enable physical and intellectual access to the site by making every attempt to assist visitors and local community in developing a keen awareness, appreciation and understanding of the remarkable palace complex. The visitors should be able to experience the City Palace as it was historically built and used - a single entity with additive layers from each era showing the architectural and social transformations of each era and its adaptive functioning as individual parts as well as a whole.

A seminal objective of the museum and its associated functions is to integrate information from living cultural traditions, with accepted scholarly and scientific methods of gathering evidence in identifying the messages that the site is to convey, in an inclusive manner. This may be ensured through a series of interventions at various levels, and communicating the messages of the site through different media with a special focus on indigenous methods. At the same time, it should be recognised that the pressures on the site need to be minimised and the visitor experience should be managed in a way that has minimal impact on the site itself. The interpretation plan aims to communicate the cultural significance of the site, especially the tradition of custodianship to all the visitors, by translating it into actual visitors' experience through a judicious selection of appropriate means of

'The Legacy of Honour' -The Mewar Sound and Light Show

interpretation. Aspects such as community participation and sustainability have also been integrated into the plan to contribute towards the ultimate goal of enabling continuity of the spirit of custodianship that the City Palace represents.

The interpretation and use of the palace is inextricably linked to the messages that the site can convey to its audience. The City Palace has been positioned as the protagonist - a living palace, an architectural ensemble showcasing a unique commitment to custodianship conveying the story of Eternal Mewar and stories of the multifaceted associations within the story. The primary and secondary themes identified are based on this structure. The protagonist, the story and the stories within together denote the cultural heritage of Eternal Mewar; the historic, environmental, social and economic contexts in the past, present and the future of the multifaceted City Palace.

The assessment of significance for the City Palace offered great insight into the interpretive themes for the City Palace. Derived from the unique continuity value along with the environmental, aesthetic, social, historical, scientific and economic values of the site, as established in the Conservation Master Plan, the primary and perhaps the most significant of the messages that the site intends to present is the 'Continuity of Custodianship and the Heritage of Eternal Mewar'. The secondary themes support the primary message and highlight the place, setting and landscape of the City Palace; the arts, artefacts and architecture of the palace, and the people, events and lifestyles associated with it. These themes became the guiding force for development of the interpretation plan. The tangible and intangible aspects that the primary theme would encompass include a historical and political timeline, the architectural evolution of the palace through each of its phases, its natural environment and the various historical and social events associated with it.

Traditional pooja being held at the Rameshwar Ghat, The Promenade

The entrance zone, currently houses the ticketing outside Badi Pol and offices, the library and research institute. This zone will continue most of its existing functions in the future, but will also provide information about the museum resources such as the Maharana Mewar Research Institute and Maharana Mewar Special Library that are accessed through the eastern gate in the entrance zone called Paiga Pol. The eastern block of the entrance zone will serve as a heritage resource centre for the museum with the research institute, library and similar proposed activities such as the building arts centre. The newly excavated catacombs further south house offices and work areas linked to these activities.

The adjoining section of the school is under the ownership of an educational trust and the school children utilise the parking in the entrance zone of the site. In an understanding and partnership with this educational trust, MMCF can utilise the

Traditional craftsmen displaying their products in the City Palace during 'Rang'

hostel block of the school for housing scholars and workshop participants during summer and winter breaks in the school. As a long term target, the school will move out of this premise since it is expanding and requires a larger area. The school land will subsequently be transferred back to MMCF and should be developed into a heritage resource centre and a research and educational zone for the museum.

The outer courtyards of Manek Chowk and Moti Chowk as well as the surrounding blocks will also realign its current use. Manek Chowk, entered through the entrance zone is the largest public space of the City Palace, and one of the most significant historically. Manek Chowk also forms the backdrop for most festivals and public events held at the City Palace. The southern end of the chowk has the Palki Khana restaurant. Manek Chowk functions quite successfully; hence the only short term change proposed here was extension of seating for the Palkikhana restaurant that has been carried out recently. In the long term, the landscaping of the entire Manek Chowk may be taken up to restore it to its original layout. The final decision regarding this intervention will be made after consulting with the various stakeholders and experts.

The courtyard of Moti Chowk historically linked the inner areas of the City Palace, and continues to serve as a central space that links the Mardana and the Zenana areas. Earlier, it was being used as a space for parking and mostly being used by the office staff, but recently the entire area was re-organised as the main entrance area to the Mardana and Zenana galleries. It now houses an open air seating area, with new stone benches and shaded seating. The audio-guide service is also provided in this *chowk*. Visitors entering through the Toran Pol see a small ticketing and information kiosk which has been recently constructed within the *chowk*. Other visitor amenities such as drinking water and restrooms have been provided in the *chowk*.

The Khasa Rasoda, which currently houses the MMCF Offices, is proposed to be an Interpretation Centre, which will communicate the themes of the site in one single space, especially to disabled and elderly visitors who may not be able to access all the spaces of the palace. The Satnavari Paiga would continue to serve as stables for horses allowing visitors to experience a historic use that has continued over the centuries. Hence, Moti Chowk is proposed to serve as an orientation centre and museum lobby from where the visitor can move into different museum galleries or thematic trails – the Mardana Mahal in the north or the Zenana Mahal in the south and access visitor amenities.

Two key issues will be addressed in Mardana and Zenana spaces through the reuse proposals; the first is bringing a large percentage of the unused spaces into regular use to ensure long term maintenance and upkeep and secondly, to assign appropriate gallery spaces to each of the zones to develop coherent and simultaneous themes for the visitor. The basic concept is to utilise the multiple levels of small architectural spaces in Mardana Mahal as a series of architectural experiences. The focus will be on architecture and the authentic depiction of eras through the architecture. The Salehkhana and Sabha Shiromani will retain their existing functions as the armoury gallery and an events space respectively. The existing lifestyle galleries such as Bhim Vilas and Pitam Niwas will be enhanced through lighting, signage and management of display. The story based display in the Nauchowki Mahal and Vani Vilas may be interpreted in a more effective manner, relating with the architectural forms and style of the space. Mor Chowk and Pitam Niwas which offer a unique insight into the royal lifestyle as well as showcasing some of the finest decorative artwork in the palace shall be made universally accessible.

Zenana Mahal has a much simpler layout than the Mardana and also bigger spaces. Additionally, it has the advantage of being spread across fewer floors, making it simpler to access. Unlike the Mardana, it has fewer architecturally extraordinary spaces and the arts and crafts used in the exteriors and interiors are also less impressive. The layout and spatial quality of the Zenana offers an opportunity to use the interiors as special galleries and collections. The Amar Mahal, which is also part of the Zenana has been restored to host a Silver Gallery titled Amar Mahal Gallery: Splendour of Silver—Reflecting the Finest of Silversmithing that showcases the impressive silver collection of the Maharanas. The challenge in the Amar Mahal galleries was to balance the conservation of spaces while maintaining international standards of museum display. Furthermore, the Amar Mahal is a series of small chambers, so evolving a simple circulation system, and providing lighting and adequate display space posed significant challenges. The exteriors and interior spaces were conserved, using traditional materials, and at the same time upgraded electrical and data services were laid out in a systematic manner.

The Photography Gallery comprises of a simple circulation system and a controlled internal environment to ensure the long term protection of the collections, which are currently being archived in the City Palace. The opening exhibition entitled 'Long Exposure: The Camera at Udaipur, 1857-1957' provided a photographic overview of the reign of five successive Maharanas of Mewar at Udaipur captured through the lingering gaze of the camera. This exhibition was based on a selection of material from the Museum archives of the Maharanas of Mewar. The archives comprise photographic materials ranging from glass-plate negatives, card photographs, photomontages, and painted photographs. Other recent galleries that have been opened up in a similar fashion are the music gallery titled Saraswati Vilas Gallery: Symphony of Mewar—A Royal Collection of Musical Instruments, showcasing traditional musical instruments, the sculpture gallery titled Som Niwas Gallery: Divine Gesture—Magnificence of Mewar Spirituality, and the curtain-raiser to the textile and costume gallery titled Gokul Niwas Gallery: The Curtain Raiser—The Mewar Regalia, Textiles and Costumes Exhibition.

The proposed reuse plan also includes thematic trails and tours through the City Palace. Apart from the regular museum itinerary, which could be self-guided, enhanced through interpretation signage and printed material, the visitor could potentially take regular gallery trails, while some galleries could have separate ticketing for a more specialised audience. A Lakeside View Trail has been devised, that passes through the Mardana and on to the Zenana terrace, addressing the site

Tripoliya before restoration

environs of the City Palace. This trail marks the locations where the visitor can get picturesque views of the surrounding areas through telescopes and interprets the same to the visitor through signage added on site. This trail would be open to all visitors and could be taken by the visitors by themselves with the aid of a brochure. An Adventure Trail for Children is also proposed, which is being designed through participation of school children engaged in a competition. The trail would be specially aimed at junior educational groups and promoted as a special package for children.

Special theme trails such as a Palace by Night Trail and themed Flora Fauna and Garden Design Trail, designed to introduce visitors to the different layers of the City Palace will be introduced. Lighting, signage and various media will become integral components of these trails. Specially trained guides will help visitors familiarise themselves with various aspects of the City Palace's art, architecture and history. A special Maharana Bhupal Singh Trail is proposed for the differently abled (ambulatory and semi-ambulatory disabilities) to interpret the site as experienced by Maharana Bhupal Singh who had ambulatory disabilities confining him to a wheel chair. This would include the Pitam Niwas and Bhupal Vilas lifestyle galleries that showcase the life style of Maharana Bhupal Singh and connect with Bhupal Prakash through special access from the lift.

Tripoliya as seen from Badi Pol

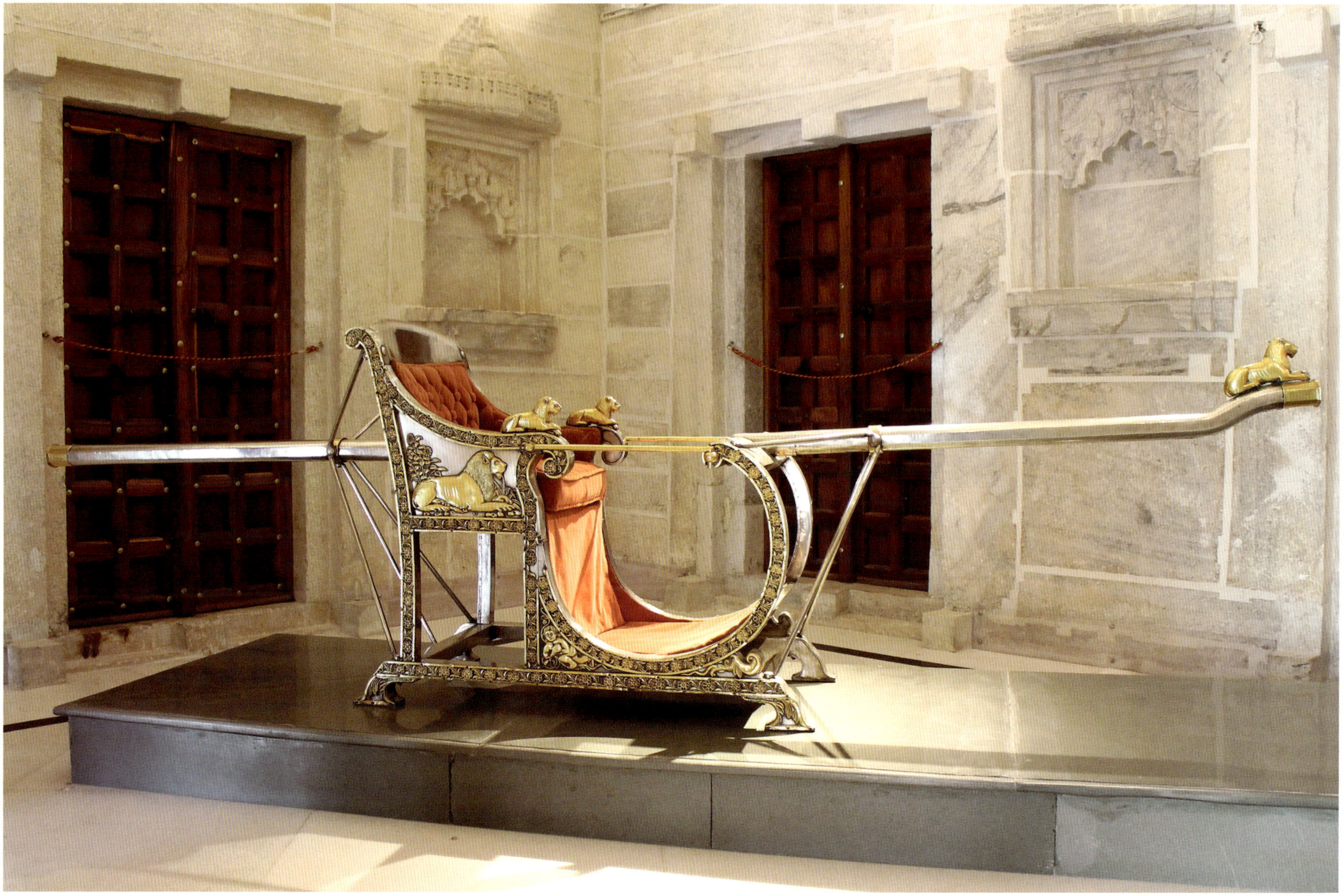

Above: Tam Jaam (Open Litter) displayed in Amar Mahal, Silver Gallery, The City Palace Museum, Udaipur, Late 19th century, Acc. No: 2014.29.0085

The various events, festivals and activities at the City Palace set it apart from other institutions as they enable the audience to connect with a site in a personal and interactive manner. These events form an integral part of the overall experience of the palace and will only be enhanced through an integrated strategy that will result in a single annual calendar communicated to a diverse visitor base. The aim of the program is to create innovative programming for enhanced visitor experience. Each festival is proposed to extend from a one day celebration into a three to five days activity that will include art and crafts market, cultural performances and training modules. The festive celebrations and activities will be publicised with adequate lead time allowing greater participation and reach. Outreach programs should cater to local, national and international needs that integrate with existing events reflecting continuity. The benefits of interpretation will percolate down to all those connected with the running of the interpretive program. Dedicated efforts will need to be made to arrange for sponsorship of large segments of the interpretive program through a cooperative venture with the local stakeholders and government bodies. The focus on identity of Mewar could be brought out to strengthen the spirit of Mewar and its association with the City Palace– enhancing the continuity value of the site. The outreach program will include specialist

Silver Horse Carriage displayed in Amar Mahal, Silver Gallery, The City Palace Museum, Udaipur, Early 20th century, Acc. No: 2014.29.0023

The Camera at Udaipur

Above: Sculptures in Som Niwas Gallery: Divine Gesture—Magnificence of Mewar Spirituality, the Zenana Mahal

Facing Page: Top A view of Bhagwat Prakash Gallery

Below Traditional musical instruments on display in the Zenana Mahal programs for researchers, educational programs and inspirational programs targeting different visitor groups. A calendar of events is already in place by the MMCF that is modified and updated annually.

To supplement the annual calendar and the new museum itineraries, several workshops have already been organised for training, collaboration and as educational exercises. The workshops planned during the making of the master plan with institutions such as architectural colleges, National Museum and UNESCO India have paved a future path for similar academic and collaborative activities that use the site as an educational resource. The most recent initiative includes the World Living Heritage Festival and Conference held in 2012, 2014 and 2016. The festival includes educational workshops between heritage professionals, the host and students; multi-disciplinary collaborative arts and crafts workshops; folklore and storytelling workshops with school students; design workshops with art and architecture students and professionals; puppet workshops with international puppeteers and traditional performers etc. One also hopes to evolve effective workshop prototypes incorporating documentation, training and capacity building and dissemination processes with the intention of fuelling the creative spark infused with excellence, innovation and freshness that sustains the living heritage of the City Palace.

Right: About the City and Lake View Trail:

The trail includes a series of vantage points within the City Palace, Udaipur offering spectacular views of its cultural landscape. The City Palace is located on the banks of the historic Lake Pichola and the Aravali hills, distinct for its breathtaking views and natural terraces, proximity to reliable source of water (Lake Pichola) and the strategic advantage it offered to the custodians of erstwhile Mewar. The trail takes one along the palace spaces that visually narrate the interaction between the natural environment and structures built by the various rulers of Mewar from 16th to early 20th century. Each point in the trail is testimony to the interaction between the society and the built structures, and captures both the tangible and intangible values that make up the cultural landscape of Udaipur city.

V1 **Chandra Mahal** (early 17th century)
The Jharoka on the western side of Chandra Mahal with its stone screens and stained glass work offers a beautiful view of Lake Pichola. Chandra Mahal also known as Rang Mahal was where the Maharana played Holi in earlier times, in the monolithic pool.

V2 **Baadi Mahal West Wing** (18th century)
It offers a wider view of the cultural landscape of Udaipur with its historic layering of the cultural and natural values. This wider context includes the lake networks, the expanse of the Aravali ranges and the city's built environment.

V3 **Mukut Mandir** (early 18th century)
Though the stone jails and hued glass work enclosing the Mukut Mandir, one can see the 17th century Jagdish Temple and the old city change its colour.

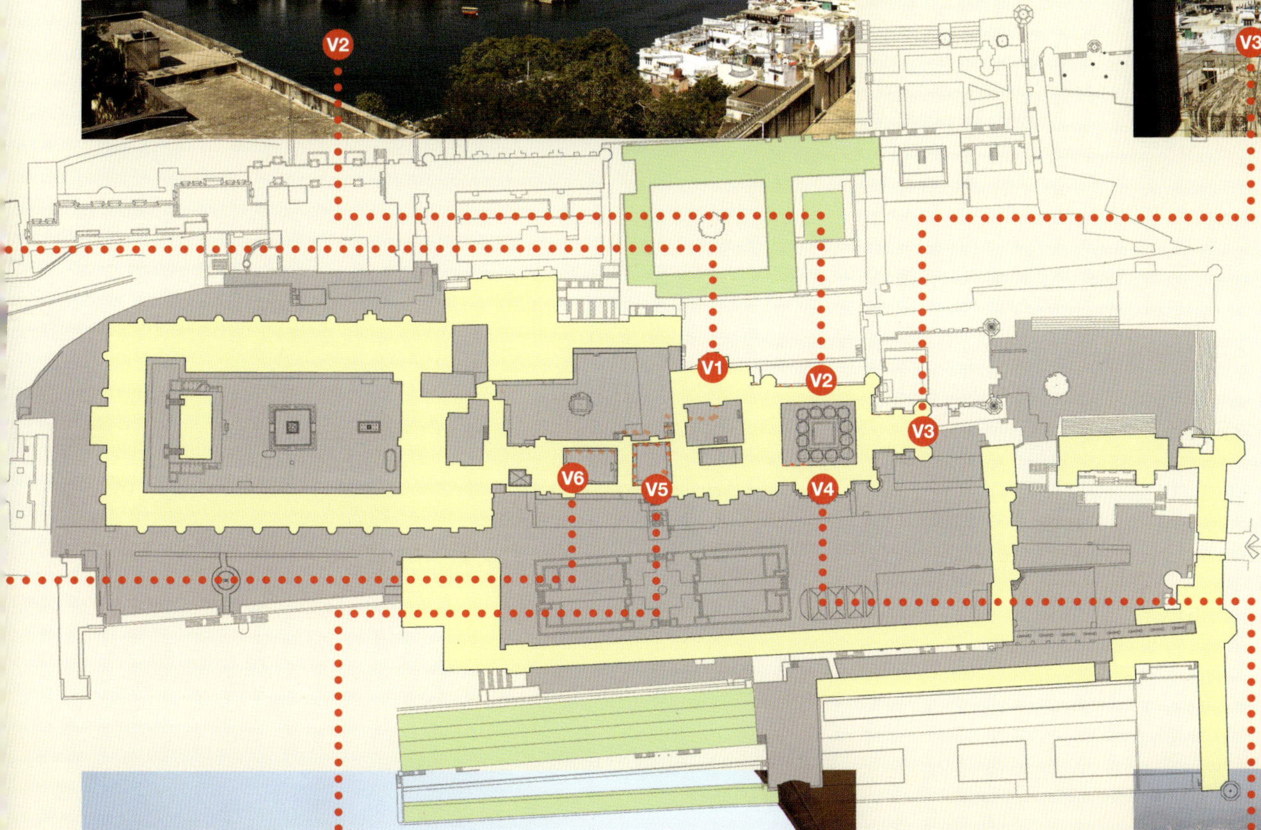

V4 Baadi Mahal - East Wing (early 18th century)
A Rajput Mughal style palatial garden with a central pool on the hilltop. It offers a view and understanding of the hierarchical layers which form the city's historical fabric; starting from the massive palace gates to the narrow street networks with old havelis and temples.

V5 Chini Chitrashali (18th–19th century)
The triple cusped arched projected Chini Jharoka, decorated with China and Delft tiles provides an excellent view of the city, Gulab Bagh (the city garden) and Machla Magra (hill used for the first fortification of the town).

V6 Surya Prakash (late 19th century)
The enclosed gallery with a series of cusped arches overlooks the Suraj Pol which had once been the main entrance to the Palace from the eastern side before the construction of Badi Pol towards the north.

Top: Students designing Children's Trail for the Museum

Right: Documentation Process: Handling, Accessioning, Measuring, Recording, Photography and Data Entry

Top: India Habitat Centre initiative 'Art in Public Spaces' with Maharana of Mewar Charitable Foundation at Jor Bagh Metro Station, New Delhi, in January 2015

Right: India Habitat Centre initiative 'Art in Public Spaces' with Maharana of Mewar Charitable Foundation at New Mandi House Metro Station, New Delhi, in October 2016

INDEX

ENTRANCE ZONE

A
A1 Badi Pol
A2 Nakkarkhana ki Chatri/ Ghadiyal ki Chatri
A3 Elephant Zone - Entrance Court (Hathiyon Ka Halqa)
A4 East wing- Torans
A5 East wing- Maharana Mewar Special Library and catacombs
A6 West wing-MMCF Trust Office
A7 West wing-Kothar

OUTER COURTYARDS

B
B1 Tripoliya and Hawa Mahal
B2 Manek Chowk
B3 East wing - Paiga and Darikhana, Hathi Aagad, Hathnal Ka Darikhana, Naharon Ka Darikhana and Nagina Badi Ka Darikhana
B4 Suraj Pol
B5 South wing - Palki Khana
B6 Toran Pol
B7 Moti Chowk
B8 West wing - Khasa Rasoda
B9 West wing - Chhota Darikhana, Sata Navari Paiga
B10 North wing - Ganesh Chowk

MARDANA MAHAL

C
C1 Mardana Deodhi and Entrance Lobby
C2 Sabha Shiromani Ka Darikhana
C3 Saleh Khana
C4 Ganesh Deodhi
C5 Rai Angan
C6 West wing first level - Nauchowki Mahal
C7 West wing second level - Chandra Mahal/ Lakhu Gokhda
C8 West wing third level - Kacheri Mahal
C9 East wing first level- Nika Ki Chopad
C10 East wing second level - Dilkhushal Mahal
C11 East wing third level - Kanch Ki Burj/ Chitram Ki Burj
C12 South wing- Service block
C13 Baadi Mahal
C14 North, West and East wing, First level- Shiv Prasana Amar Vilas
C15 North wing, Second Level- Mukut Mandir
C16 East wing- Yash Mandir
C17 Badi Chitrashali
C18 North wing, First level- Sat Tanka/ Kishan Vilas, Chini Jharokha, Vani Vilas, Madan Vilas
C19 The Mor Chowk
C20 East wing, First level- Swarup Vilas
C21 South wing, First level- Surya Chopad
C22 South wing, Second level- Pitam Niwas
C23 North wing, First level- Manek Mahal
C24 North wing, Second level- Moti Mahal, Bhim Vilas

ZENANA MAHAL

D
D1 Zenana Deodhi
D2 Bhandar Chowk
D3 East wing, First level- Amar Mahal
D4 East wing, Second level- Sarbat Vilas
D5 South wing, First and Second level
D6 Lakshmi Chowk
D7 North wing, Second level- Bhupal Vilas
D8 East wing, First level- Zenana Mahal Palace
D9 South wing, First level- Zenana Mahal Palace
D10 West wing, First level- Zenana Mahal Palace, new kitchen wing, Bhupal Prakash
D11 Chowmukha
D12 Pitamberai ji ka Chowk

SITE SURROUNDINGS

E
E1 East wing- Maharana Mewar Public School
E2 South wing- Chandra Chowk
E3 West wing- Khush Mahal Ka Chowk
E4 West wing- Karan Vilas
E5 West wing- Rokdda Ka Bhandar
E6 West wing- Khush Mahal

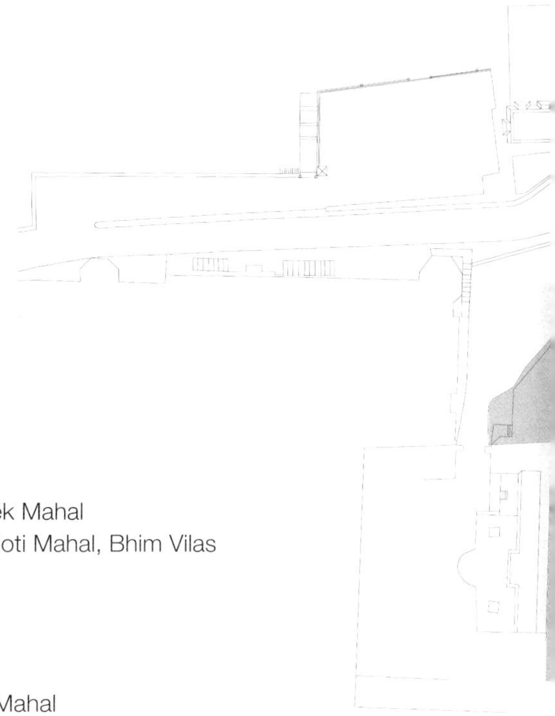

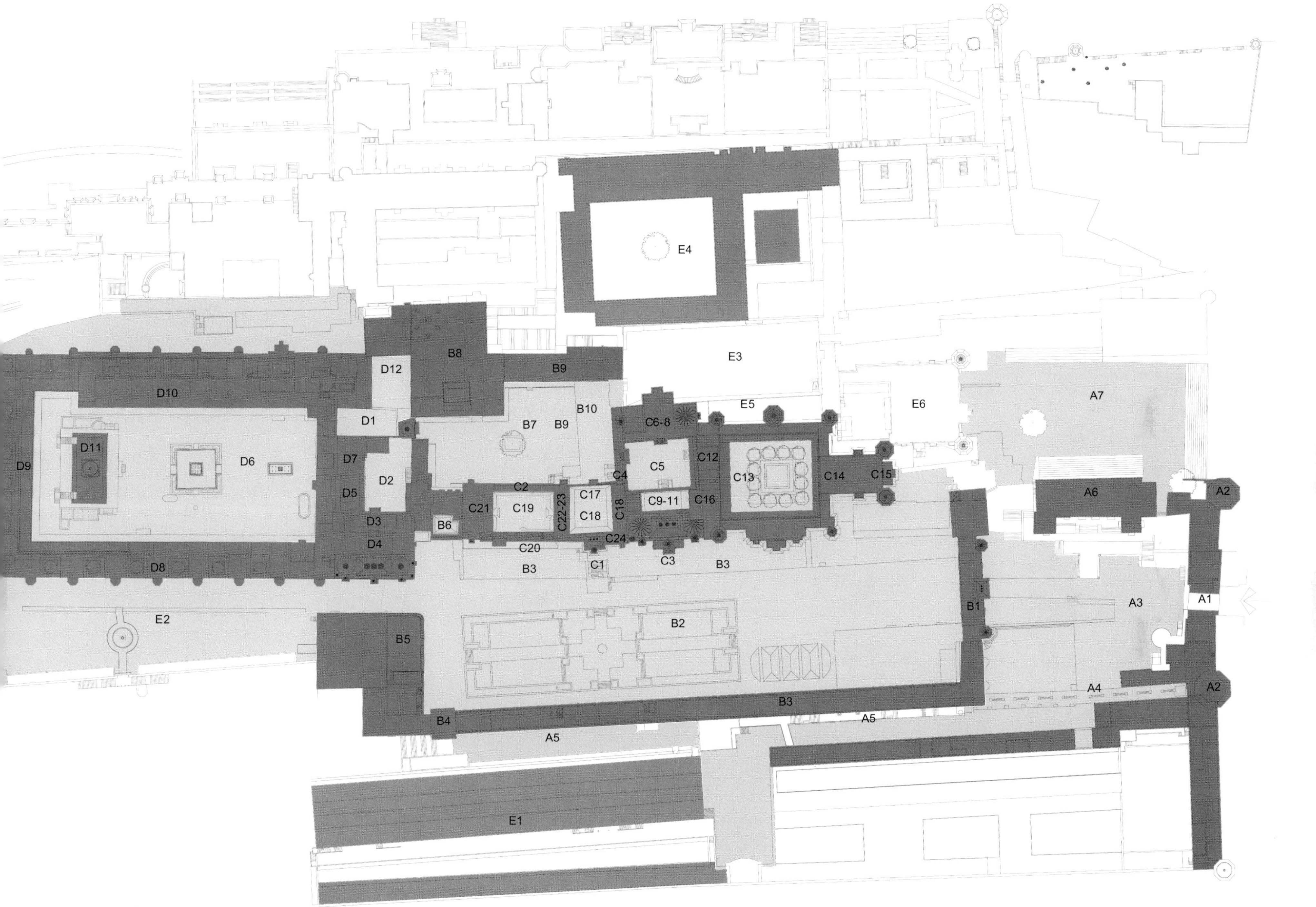

LEGEND

- Built space
- Open space
- Site surroundings

Bibliography

Primary Sources

I. Overview of the Literary and Visual archives (Sixteenth – Nineteenth century)

In Mewar, the Sanskrit literary tradition flourished during the reign of Rana Amar Singh II (1698-1710 AD), with Pandit Jiwadhar, the author of the 'Amarsar', among those at the Mewar Court. Another important text of this period was the 'Amar Bhushan' - a treatise on astronomy. In the reign of Maharana Jagat Singh I (1628 - 1652 AD), Pandit Mohan Bhatt wrote the 'Jagat Simhastaka,' Raghunath the 'Jagat Singh Kavya', and Lakshmi Nath composed the famous 'Jagannath Rai Temple Inscription'. Litterateurs at Maharana Raj Singh's (1653 - 1680 AD) Court included not just Ranchod Bhatt, author of the 'Amar Kavya Vamshavali' and 'Raj Prashasti Mahakavya' etc, and Pandit Sada Shiva - who had come to Mewar from Kashi (Banaras), but also Dhundhi Raj, who wrote the 'Raj Ratnakar' about gems. Man Kavi, who completed the 'Raj-Vilas' in 1680, and Pt. Mukund who wrote the 'Raj Simbastaka', also flourished at Raj Singh's Court. Kishordas's 'Raj Prakash', Shrilal Bhatt's 'Raj Singh Varanam' and Mukund Das's 'Raj Singhsatak' are other works written during the period of Raj Singh. Among important literary works of the eighteenth century one was the Braj text, 'Jag-Vilas,' of Nand Ram, describing the life and Court of Jagat Singh II of Mewar. The scions of this southern Indian family that settled at Udaipur included the well-acclaimed litterateurs Ranchhod Bhatt, Ram Chandra and Babu Bhatt.

In the nineteenth century, Maharana Sajjan Singh also established the 'Sajjan Vani Vilas' library. It was during Sajjan Singh's reign that Kaviraj Shyamaldas (1836-1893), who was appointed to look after this library, wrote the major part of his now-renowned history of Mewar. The title of 'Kaviraj', or 'King of Poets', was bestowed on Shyamaldas for his skills. He is best-known for his five-volume history of Mewar - the 'Veer Vinod', published by Mewar State in 1886, then suppressed, and finally released for public consumption in 1945.

II. City Palace Museum and Maharana Mewar Research Institute, Udaipur

Sixteenth – Early Twentieth century Paintings collection at the City Palace Museum, Udaipur

Bahidas, daily records of the rulers, from the mid eighteenth century to the twentieth century maps from the early twentieth century. Besides the above mentioned literary texts, the large eighteenth – early twentieth century miniature paintings of the Udaipur depicting court histories amongst its palatial spaces have been utilized to their maximum potential to understand the development of Udaipur's palace complex. The above described set of primary documents was referred primarily within the archives and libraries of the City Palace Museum and Maharana Mewar Research Institute at Udaipur. Additionally, primary research material was collated at national and state level archives, such as the Rajasthan State Archives, Bikaner, Rajasthan Oriental Research Institute, Udaipur, Pratap Shodh Sansthaan, Udaipur, City Palace Museum, Jaipur, National Museum, New Delhi, and the American Institute of Indian Studies, Gurgaon.

Research within international venues, such as the James Tod Collection in the Royal Asiatic Society, London also yielded important manuscripts. International Collections of Mewar paintings housed within the National Gallery of Victoria, Melbourne, Metropolitan Museum, New York, and the Victoria and Albert Museum, London were researched through published catalogues and a visit was made to the San Diego Museum of Art in San Diego, California that has 72 Mewar miniature paintings from the Edward Binney collection.

Secondary Sources

I. Books and Articles

Alimuddin, (2001) Mewar ka Ithihaas, Pratap Shodh Pratishthan, Bhupal Nobles Sansthan, Udaipur.

Andhare, Shridhar (1987) Chronology of Mewar Paintings, Agam Kala Prakashan, Delhi.

Austin, Ian (1999) Mewar the World's Longest Serving Dynasty, Lustre Press, Roli Books.

Bhati, Hukum Singh (1994) Mewar Rawal Ranaji Ri Baat, Pratap Shodh Pratishtan, Bhupal Nobels Sansthan, Udaipur.

Bahura, GN and Chanramani Singh (1990) Catalogue of Historical Documents in Kapad-dwara, Jaipur, Maps and Plans. City Palace Museum, Jaipur

Bhatt, Rajendra Shankar (1976) Udai Singh, Pratap Singh, Amar Singh – Mewar ke Maharana aur Shanshah Akbar, Saftiq Sansthan, Jaipur.

Chundawat, Padamshree Laxmi kumari, (2002) Tabara ri Batan ar Hukaro Do Sa, Chirag Prakashan, Udaipur.

Daljeet, Mathur V.K., Shah, Rajeshwari (2003) Fragrance in Colour, National Museum, New Delhi.

Davenport, Hugh (1975) The Trials and Triumphs of the Mewar Kingdom, Approved by Maharana of Mewar Charitable Foundation, Udaipur.

Erskine, K.D. (1992; reprint 1904) Rajputana Gazetteers-The Mewar Residency, Vintage Books.

Hiran, Roopa (2002) Udaipur History and Heritage, Meera Publications, Udaipur.

Jugnu, Shrikrishna (2004) Maharana Pratap ka Darbari Pandit Chakrapani Mishr aur Samarak Samiti, Udaipur.

Jugnu, Shrikrishna (2004) Rajvallabha Vastusastram of Sutradhara Mandana: A Treatise on Housing, Architecture and Astrology, Parimal Publication.

Kerr, J. S. (2000) The Conservation Plan, National Trust of Australia (NSW), fifth edition.

Khera, Dipti and Mansukhani, Raju (2002) The City Within a City – Vol. I: Jagmandir on Lake Pichola, Penguin Enterprise by Penguin Books India.

Kothari, Dev, (1985) Ranchod Bhatt Pranitam Amarkavyam, Sahitya Sansthan, Rajasthan Vidyapeeth, Udaipur.

Kothari, Dev (1989) Kishana Adha's Bhim Vilas (Historical and Biographical Epic on Maharana Bhim Singh of Mewar), Sahitya Sansthan, Rajasthan Vidyapeeth, Udaipur.

Kothari, Dev (1991) Maharana Pratap aur Unka Yug, Sahitya Sansthan, Rajasthan Vidyapeeth, Udaipur.

Masters, Brian (1990) Maharana the Story of the Rulers of Udaipur, Mapin Publishing Pvt. Ltd. Ahemdabad.

Matero, Frank (Spring 2000) "Ethics and Policy in Conservation" Newsletter 15.1. Getty Conservation Institute. LA

Meininger, Irmgard (2000) City Palace of Udaipur, D.K. Printworld (Pvt.) Ltd., New Delhi.

Menaria, Motilal (reprint1983) Mahakavi Ranchod Bhatta Pranitam Rajprasastih Mahakavyam, Sahitya Sansthan Rajsthan Vidyapeeth, Udaipur.

Ojha, Raibhadur Gaurishankar Heerachand (1994) Udaipur Rai ka Ithihas, Rajasthani Granthagar, Jodhpur.

Paliwal, Devilal (1985) Mewar Rajvansha ki Raniyon, Kunwaron aur Kunwariyon ka Hal, Sahitya Sansthan, Rajasthan Vidhyapeeth, Udaipur.

Paliwal, Devilal (2000) Maharana Pratap Samriti Granth, Sahitya Sansthan Vidhyapeeth, Udaipur.

Pandey, Lalit (2005) Yug Yugin Mewar, Institute of Rajasthan Studies, Sahitya Sansthan Udaipur.

Pandya, Shailja (2001; reprint?) Shri Sutradharmandanvirachit Rajvallabhamandanam Hindivyokhaypatam, Chowkhamba Surbharti Prakashan, Varanasi.

Pinhey, A.F. (1909) History of Mewar, Books Treasure, Jodhpur.

Ranawat, Ishwar Singh (2004) Rajasthan ke Jal Sansadhan, Chirag Prakashan, Udaipur.

Ranawat, Manohar Singh, (2003; reprint) Chittor-Udaipur ka Patnama (Mewar ka Itihas) Part 1, Shri Natnagar Shodh Sansthan, Sitamau.

Ranawat, Manohar (2003; reprint) Chittor-Udaipur ka Patnama (Mewar ka Ithihas Vol II), Shri Natnagar Shodh Sansthan.

Ranawat, Manohar Singh (dates?) Munot Nancy ki Khayat Bhag I, Shri Natnagar Shodh Sansthan.

Ranawat, Saajan (2002) Maharana Pratap Se Sambandit Satrot Aiwam Sthan Maharana Pratap Samrat Samiti, Udaipur.

Sharma, G.N. (1954) Mewar and the Mughal Emperors, Shivalal Agarwal and Co. (Pvt.) Ltd. Agra.

Sharma, G.N. (1992) Haqiqat Bahida – 1 H.H. Maharana Fateh Singhji of Udaipur (24 Dec. 1884 to 24 May 1930), Maharana Mewar Research Institute Palace, Udaipur

Sharma, G.N. (1994) Haqiqat Bahida – 2 to 6 H.H. Maharana Fateh Singhji of Udaipur (24 Dec. 1884 to 24 May 1930) Vol. II, Maharana Mewar Research Institute Palace, Udaipur

Sharma, G.N. (1997) Haqiqat Bahida –7 to 16 H.H. Maharana Fateh Singhji of Udaipur (24 Dec. 1884 to 24 May 1930) Vol. III, Maharana Mewar Research Institute Palace, Udaipur

Sharma, G.N. (1996) Haqiqat Bahida – 17 to 26 H.H. Maharana Fateh Singhji of Udaipur (24 Dec. 1884 to 24 May 1930) Vol. IV, Maharana Mewar Research Institute Palace, Udaipur

Sharma, G.N. (1997) Haqiqat Bahida – 27 to 37 H.H. Maharana Fateh Singhji of Udaipur (24 Dec. 1884 to 24 May 1930) Vol. V, Maharana Mewar Research Institute Palace, Udaipur

Singh, Devaki (2000) Charities of the House of Mewar, The Maharana Mewar Historical

Publication Trust, The City Palace, Udaipur.

Singh, Kesri (2006) Maharana Pratap The Hero of Haldi ghati, Books Treasure, Jodhpur. Somani, Ramvallabh, Veer Bhoomi Chittor, Chirag Prakashan, Udaipur.

Talbot, Cynthia (2007) "The Mewar Court's Construction of History," in William, Joanna. Kingdom of the Sun: Indian Court and Village Art from the Princely State of Mewar. Asian Art Museum of San Francisco, San Francisco.

Tanwar, Dhayabhai Tulsinath (1982) Sansmaran-Maharana Fateh Singhji, Maharana Bhupal Singhji, Maharana Bhagwat Singhji Mewar, Shree Git Printing Press, Udaipur.

Tillotson, G.H.R. (1987 Yale University) (1999 In India) The Rajput Palaces – the Development of Architectural Style 1450-1750, Oxford University Press, London.

__________, (1998) "Painting and Understanding Mughal Architecture". In Paradigms of Indian Architecture: Space and Time in Representation and Design, 59-79, ed. G.H.R. Tillotson. Curzon, London.

Tod, James. (1997; Reprint from 1829, 32) Annals and Antiquities of Rajasthan, or, the Central and Western Rajpoot States of India. Vol I-II. Rupa & Co, New Delhi.

Topsfield, Andrew. (2001) "City Palace and Lake Palaces: Architecture and Court Life in Udaipur

Painting." Stones in the Sand: The Architecture of Rajasthan. Ed. Giles (G.H.R.) Tillotson. Marg Publications, Mumbai.

__________. (1990) City Palace Museum, Udaipur. Mapin Publishing, Ahmedabad.

__________. (2001) Court Painting at Udaipur: Art Under the Patronage of the Maharanas of Mewar.

Zurich: Museum Rietberg in association with Artibus Asiae Publishers.

__________. (1980) Paintings from Rajasthan in the National Gallery of Victoria. National Gallery of Victoria, Melbourne.

Vyas, Rajshekhar (1988) Mewar ki Kala Aur Sthapatya, Rajasthan Prakashan, Jaipur.

William, Joanna (2007) Kingdom of the Sun: Indian Court and Village Art from the Princely State of Mewar. Asian Art Museum of San Francisco, San Francisco.

Zaveri, Parul and Patel, Nimish (2001) "Traditional values and Architectural Understanding". In Stones in the Sand: The Architecture of Rajasthan, 112-121. Ed. Giles (G.H.R.) Tillotson. Marg Publications, Mumbai.

II. Charters

(2007) The ICOMOS Ename Charter. The ICOMOS Charter for the Interpretation and Presentation of Cultural Heritage Sites. Proposed Final Draft

(2004) Principles for the Conservation of Heritage Sites in China Los Angeles: Getty Conservation Institute.

(2004) The Charter for the conservation of unprotected architectural heritage and sites in India India: INTACH.

(1999) Burra Charter Australia: ICOMOS

III. Reports

Jeff Sheppard Heritage Consultants (December 2003) Curango Historic Precinct: Conservation,

Interpretation and Management Plan

Cambridge Architectural Research Ltd (October. 2006) Final Draft of the Conservation Plan for the National Maritime Museum.

Clive Lucas, Stapleton and Partners Pty. Ltd. (Oct. 2005) The Australia Museum, Sydney, Final Report of the Conservation Management Plan.

Godden Mackay Context (March 2000) Port Arthur Historic Site Overview Report. Conservation Plan – Volume 1. Prepared for Port Arthur Historic Site Management Authority

____________(March 2000) Port Arthur Historic Site Supporting Information. Conservation Plan – Volume 2. Prepared for Port Arthur Historic Site Management Authority

Mason, Ranadall (2002) "Assessing values in Conservation Planning: Methodological Issues and Choices".

Assessing the Values of Cultural Heritage', Research Report of The Getty Conservation Institute, Los Angeles

_____________(2002). Assessing the Values of Cultural Heritage', Research Report of The Getty

Conservation Institute, Los Angeles

Nottingham City Council (2002) Conservation Plan for Wollaton Hall and Park

de La Torre, Matia(Ed.) (2002) Assessing the Values of Cultural Heritage. Research Report for the Getty Conservation Institute.

IV. Consultants' Reports

MGML Pvt. Ltd. (2004) City Palace Museum, Udaipur Report

Bardhan, Suchandra (2006) Report on the City Palace Complex- Landscape research, documentation, analysis and proposed landscape policies

Batul F Raj (2006) City Palace Museum Facilities Planning Report

Jain, Shikha (2006) City Palace Complex-Architectural Evolution, Management and Use analysis and Use Policies

Kanwal, Cheena (2006) Report on the City Palace Complex- Environmental research, analysis and proposed environmental policies

Khare, Ajay (2006) Condition Assessment of Built Fabric, Issues and Polices

Karkaria, Dhun (2007) An Interpretive Idea for the City Palace Complex, Udaipur

IIT Roorkee (2006) Photogrammetry Report

Index

Dates given under the portraits of the Maharanas in this book indicate their reigning periods.

Glossary

Arraish: *Finish in lime and marble powder and ground seashells*
Arhat: *Persian wheel for drawing water*

Baori: *Step-well*
Baithak: *Sitting space*
Bahida: *Daily record of the Ruler*
Bailkhano: *Stables for bullocks*
Baadi: *Garden*
Brahmin: *A person who belongs to the uppermost or highest caste, originally that of priests.*
Brahmini: *A lady who belongs to the uppermost or highest caste, originally that of priests.*
Bael: *Aegle marmelos, is considered sacred by Hindus. It has medicinal properties.*

Chowk: *A four-sided courtyard*
Chopad: *Covered spaces opening into a court*
Chitrashali: *Semi-covered painted galleries for the rulers to use as leisure galleries*
Chhajja: *Projected shading device*
Chatri: *A sort of vaulted dome*
Chehebcha: *An artificial pond or pool structure*
Charan: *A Bard or a minstrel*

Durbar: *Royal Court*
Deodhi: *Smaller Gateways that demarcate transition spacesinto smaller or more private courtyards*
Darikhanas: *Gathering space for ruler and nobles*
Dalan: *Platform*
Dhuni: *Fire-pit*
Daftar: *Office*
Deewan-i-Khas: *Space for entertaining special guests*
Deewan-i-Aam: *Space for receiving outsiders*

Ekantars: *a brief of a Baheda*

Farman: *A document recording the Emperor's command or order/ Royal Decree*

Gokhda: *Projected window*
Gaddi: *Throne*
Ghat: *Embankment with steps*

Hathi ki Agad: *Space for elephant fight*
Holi: *Hindu festival of colours*

Jethi: *Wrestler*
Jaali: *Lattice screen window*
Jharokha: *Projected and screened window*

Kalash: *Finial*
Kullar: *Small clay tubes*
Kothar: *Storage space*
Khamira: *Lime wash*
Khana: *Room or space*

Mahal: *Palatial rooms usually on the upper level*
Mandir: *Temple*
Mardana: *Men's quarters*
Magra: *Hillock*
Mehendi: *Henna*

Nakkara: *drum*
Naqqarkhana: *Space for playing drums near the entrance gate*
Niwas: *Place of stay*
Naginabaadi: *A Mughal style garden*
Nauchowki: *Nine grid square room*
Neem: *Azadirachta Indica, also known as Neem, Nimtree, and Indian Lilac. It has medicinal properties.*

Osara: *Semi-covered veranda space forprayers and rituals*
Ovari: *Small storage room*

Pol: *Entrance Gateway*
Pal: *Embankment*
Panera: *Water storage space*
Prathishthan: *Foundation ceremony*
Palki: *Traditional covered carriages used to carry royal ladies and brides or palanquin*
Prakash: *Place of stay*
Paiga: *Stables area for horses*

Qazi: *Muslim Priest*

Rawla: *Palace of the queens and her coterie*
Rajvallabh: *Traditional architecture treatise of Mewar*
Rasoda: *Kitchen*
Rahat: *Persian wheel for drawing water*

Sutradhar: *Architect*
Sarai: *A resting place or inn*
Shilalekh: *Inscription found in foundation stone*
Suryavanshis: *Born from the Sun*
Shehnai: *A piped musical instrument*

Toran: *Temporary crown tied to the entrance gate*
Tula Daan: *Donation measured in weight of ruler*
Tulsi: *Basil (Sacred plant for Hindus)*
Tulsibedi: *Space for sacred basil plant*

Vilas: *Place of stay*

Yajna: *Fire Ritual of Hindus*

Zenana: *Women's quarters*

Acknowledgements

THE TEAM

Principal Consultants
Development and Research Organization for Nature, Arts and Heritage (DRONAH)
Shikha Jain - Project Supervisor
Ajay Khare - Conservation Consultant
Cheena Kanwal - Environment Consultant
Parul Munjal - Conservation Architect
Rima Hooja - History & Archaeology Consultant
Suchandra Bardhan - Landscape Consultant

Documentation, Compilation and Design Team, DRONAH
Conservation Architect
Somya Johri
Tapasya Samal
Vanicka Arora

Consultants for Secondary Plans
Ajit Rao- Interpretation
Manav Bhargava - Lighting
Mrinalini Bangaroo - Art Restoration (Wall Murals)
Nambankar Gupta - Management
Rohit Jigyasu - Risk Management
S Girikumar - Art Conservation (All Artifacts and works of art in situ)
Sandeep Munjal and Savita Sharma - Heritage Tourism

MMCF Staff
Bhupendra Singh Auwa - Administrator in Chief
Mayank Gupta - Deputy Secretary MMCF - Development
D B Acharya - Chief Engineer MMCF - Projects
Nikhil Tamboli - Assistant Architect MMCF - Projects
Prashant Lohar - Archives and Conservation Assistant, MAMM, MMCF

MMCF Resource
Dipti Khera
Alka Pande
Deepthi Sasidharan
Pramod Kumar KG
Mrinalini Venkateswaran

DRONAH Team
Hemani Badyal
Uttara Dasgupta
Shelja Bisht
Anjali

Publication Design Concept and Layout, Designflyover (DFO)
Shreya Sarda - Design Director
Avani Rajesh, Bhavik Shah, Mihir Bankapure, Santhoshram E N, Uttara Sivadas